I Will be Home in 20 Minutes

Roslyn Bell

BALBOA.
PRESS

A DIVISION OF HAY HOUSE

Balboa Press books may be ordered through booksellers or by contacting:

Balboa Press
A Division of Hay House
1663 Liberty Drive
Bloomington, IN 47403
www.balboapress.com
1-(877) 407-4847

Because of the dynamic nature of the Internet, any Web addresses or links contained in this book may have changed since publication and may no longer be valid. The views expressed in this work are solely those of the author and do not necessarily reflect the views of the publisher, and the publisher hereby disclaims any responsibility for them.

The author of this book does not dispense medical advice or prescribe the use of any technique as a form of treatment for physical, emotional, or medical problems without the advice of a physician, either directly or indirectly. The intent of the author is only to offer information of a general nature to help you in your quest for emotional and spiritual well-being. In the event you use any of the information in this book for yourself, which is your constitutional right, the author and the publisher assume no responsibility for your actions.

Any people depicted in stock imagery provided by Thinkstock are models, and such images are being used for illustrative purposes only. Certain stock imagery © Thinkstock.

ISBN: 978-1-4525-0138-3 (sc)
ISBN: 978-1-4525-0139-0 (e)

Library of Congress Control Number: 2010918052

Printed in the United States of America

Balboa Press rev. date: 2/25/2011

Contents

Introduction

I am truly humbled to tell my story in this book. At the age of 43 I have had the privilege of great gifts in life and wonderful lessons. As I now come to the other side, I am sharing them with you so that you might not feel alone in your pain or tragedy or to help you understand a loved one or friend who has experienced pain. Most of all, my story is to make you realize that your darkest days are your greatest gifts and that life is not about how many obstacles are thrown at you, but how you rise to your challenges and react to them.

It has amazed me when I recollect my life in this book. How I built hopes and dreams and turned them into reality and then within seconds an accident changed your life from joy and happiness to a brush with death. The aftermath of those few seconds, took me over a decade to recover. The utter devastation and challenges took me to very dark places. Yet when, looking back I realised that I tapped into that inner strength I never knew I had, to help me somehow to get through each day. As I tried to recover and put my life together each time I got up with wobbly legs like bambi, some other trauma took me down. Each time I was having to dig deeper to find the courage and then the final blow of cervical cancer give me the courage to stand up take my own power, rising myself like a phoenix from the ashes and build myself business' that I could only ever dreamt of.

There are laws of this Universe we live in that we never query. We take for granted that every morning it gets light and every night it gets dark. As the tide comes in, it also goes out. I have learned that your life is the same full of ups and downs. If you are having a bad day then you will know you can look forward to a good day and appreciate it when it arrives. Life has sent me some big lessons and challenges, but from this I can understand what has happened and process them. From these lessons of life you have a choice. You can either learn from them and take responsibility for yourself or lie down and become a victim. From this statement I mean, it is not what actually happens to you but how you react to it that really matters in life. The choice is yours become a Victim or rise, Victorious!

My grandmother was a wonderful resilient woman and made a big impression on my life at a very young age. She always told me, "Keep your chin up, should your belly touch the ground". Which means hold your head up not matter what happens, as you are the only person in charge of your own destiny.

This little sentence has stuck in my subconscious mind and will last my lifetime.

I thank you for giving me the opportunity to share my journey. I hope that you will find something within this book that you can connect with and be inspired to look inside yourself. Appreciate the beautiful being you are, and go and live your dream, the life you were destined to live.

CHAPTER ONE

Young & Innocent

I came from a family of six children. Four girls and Two boys. I was the second eldest. We lived in a small village called "Glenanne" (which is in Northern Ireland about 100miles from Belfast heading south) in a close-knit community where everyone knew each other. There was a primary school in the village, a shop, postoffice and a linen factory. A lot of people who lived in the village were employed in the Factory my dad was as a young boy but later ventured out into business himself. My mother worked in ladies' fashions although, became a housewife after my arrival.

My elder sister was very shy and would not venture to anything other than school until I was old enough to accompany her. As for me, a year and a half her junior, I could not wait to grow up, I was excited to get out there into the real world - it was a big adventure to me.

My earliest memory of my quest for excitement was when I was Three years old. I couldn't wait to go to school. Every day my older sister would get all dressed and go off to school to write and draw pictures. She even had a school bag, pencil case and a reading book. I so wished I could go instead of staying at home with mummy and the baby. So I made a plan, most mornings after My older sister went to school I would go and visit my grandmother who just lived a few houses away. On one particular morning I decided to take action. I got my slippers on, red with a zip up the front and didn't brush my hair, as I was in a hurry. I had more important things to do! I rushed out the front door as my mum watched me (as she always did) until I reached Granny's door. That morning I opened it very quietly and went in, then waited until I thought mum would have gone back into the house, content that I was safe at Granny's. But I had other plans. I gently opened Granny's door and crept back out. I ran up to the hedge that ran all the way across the front of our garden all the time crouching down below the hedge in case my mum would be looking out and see me. I then made my way up to the entrance path to our house, dashed across that to the end of the row of houses, and turned right up the school path, through the gate and into the playground. I didn't stop for a breath until I reached the big entrance door. I was so excited with my heart pounding in my chest. I can still remember thinking, "I have made it!" With a bit of difficulty I opened the big heavy door and entered into the silence of the corridor, walked past the cloakrooms for the girls and then the boys. I stopped for a minute to admire the coats on the hooks and wished I had one on them.

When I got to My older sister's classroom, my heart was pounding even more. Before I knew it I had opened the door and was standing just inside it, frozen to the spot. The teacher came over; she knew who I was. She took me by the hand and give me a chair beside my sister. Then she give me a pencil and a piece of paper… OH! was I in heaven. I was so pleased with myself! I was drawing like the others and having a wonderful time, but when you are enjoying yourself it always goes too quickly. Before very long there was a knock on the door. It was my mum, who was relieved to find me, sitting beside my sister with my slippers on and my hair not brushed. I remember feeling as if my bubble had burst when my mother signalled with her finger that I was to go home with her. My first adventure was over.

At age seven I joined the Brownies, my older sister was who was eight and a half by then and still shy, waited until I was old enough to join and we started together. By this time I had mastered going on lots of adventures on my own and now I was more than happy to take her by the hand. I had now progressed from going out on my own to having the responsibility of taking someone with me.

The day arrived and again as with everything in my life it seemed like another big conquest. My mum drove us both in the car to the neighbouring village of Mountnorris, where the Brownies meetings were held. When she parked the car, we got out. She said "Come on, girls" at that moment, my sister slipped her hand in mine and I told her it would be fun, but my legs were shaking and my heart was thumping with excitement and nerves, at what would be happening in this big hall we were about to enter. When we got into the hall, it seemed bigger than it looked outside, and all the girls were standing in rows in their uniforms of brown dresses. At this point even I felt scared; I did not know anyone and there just seemed to be so many of them, all lined up. The teacher came up to us, introduced herself, had a quick chat with my mum, and gently took us by the hand to the front of the rows. She announced to everyone that we had just joined and to welcome us. She then directed us to the end of a row of girls, which we later found out to be a patrol, or team. Each patrol had a name and ours was Primrose. At the Brownies we learned lots of things - sewing, knitting, cooking, camping, and badge work that gave you a sense of achievement.

Now as I write this book I am amazed to realise that as young as the age of three and seven I was owning my responsibility. These examples such as the fear of taking my sister and being responsible for her mixed with the exhilaration of joining the Brownies, making new friends and experiencing new ventures were the small shoots of how I would handle the rest of my life. Reflecting back these actions were the baby steps, the foundation of the true me. I was tapping into my inner being, my life path not only being able to push outside my comfort zone but as soon it felt comfortable, I would encourage others to do the same. Children automatically express themselves, but they also are watching their adults and peers for acceptance of their expression if this is acknowledged in a negative way this can impact on their thoughts. It is called conditioning, where the child changes its thought pattern to match that of the adult. Not all experiences in our childhood are positive but it is not what has happened to us in these experiences but how we react and use them that matters.

For Example in the early 1970's it was traditional to dress your children of the same sex in the same clothes. That was a big problem for me as my older and younger sister's body shapes were straight up and down and they had dark hair. I was the complete opposite, blonde and chubby with a tummy that stuck out and also my bottom. One particular Christmas Mum dressed us all in trendy red wet-look skirts and matching waistcoat, which tied at the front. Underneath we had a white frilly blouses and white tights. My sisters' looked beautiful but I had a problem or two! Where the waistcoat on my sisters' just touched the waistband of there skirts, mine unfortunately produced a big gap in the middle, as my tummy pushed the waistcoat up and the waistband of my skirt down, so the bottom of my blouse did not stay tucked in my skirt. Also, as the waistcoat was pushed up, it in turn pushed the frills of the blouse right up to almost under my chin. I felt like I was being suffocated in frills. To top it off my tights kept falling down! Mum spent that Christmas Day fixing my outfit. The longer she spent, the more exasperated she became. She said "Look at the state of you, the other girls are lovely". I sucked every word my mum said deep into my subconscious mind. I believed her, as all children do. I started to notice and think about everything that was being said and analysing myself in comparison to my sisters. My mind translated this as "My sisters are beautiful and I am a mess". Looking back those words had a profound effect on me and it is important for us to realise the power of our spoken word around children. Mum never meant me any harm. She was just frustrated. But as I played the words over and over in my mind I kept looking for all the things that were wrong with me. It gave me a very low self- esteem; when comparing myself to other girls, however, every lesson is a gift. I would use this gift later in my life when I opened my ladies boutique. To connect with all the women who felt the same.

As I grew up I continued challenging myself. This zest for life was growing with me and at the age of 16 I decided I wanted financial freedom and money for myself. When mum was getting her shopping one Saturday in the nearby town of Markethill I went into the chemist and asked to speak with the owner. He was a big tall man and I was a bit frightened and daunted when he approached me and asked me how he could help. I just seemed to blurt out that I was looking for a job on Saturdays and during school holidays, as at this age during the week I was doing a secretarial course at Newry College, which was about 20 miles from my home. He replied that he had no job available at the present but he would put my name on a list. Every day I would dream of working at the chemist, and every Saturday I would go in and have a walk around and imagine myself working there. It was not long until a girl who lived nearby called at my house to give me a message from the owner that he had a job available if I was interested. The following week I was there, working behind the counter serving customers, and at 6pm when I was leaving I had my first official pay packet. I was so proud of myself. This was the start of my own independence.

I gained a lot of knowledge while I worked in the chemist like how to read prescriptions, and what various medicines were for. I also liked the interaction with the other girls, and I made new friends. Even though it was fun and I really enjoyed working there, my aspiration at the time was to be a secretary - Like JR Ewing's secretary in "Dallas", the hit American television series at the time. Yes, that was what I wanted and I set my dream again.

Around this time Ivan arrived in my life. It was all very young and innocent. I was sixteen years old and Ivan was eighteen he was good looking, tall, with muscles and naturally tan skin. He lived in Newtownhamilton about 10 miles south of my house. Rode a motorbike and I was just waiting for my opportunity to get on the back. Although my mother had told me not to, I was eager to try this out. One Sunday night he asked me would I like a ride on his bike, even though I had a skirt on. Without another word I pulled it up enough to put my leg over the seat, and climbed on the back of the bike. This was the devilish or fun side of me. It was fabulous to be free, speeding along the road with the wind in my hair(no crash helmet!) with the boy that I thought was hot!. I had been observing him for a while and this was making me very happy. He drove fast; it all seemed exhilarating to me.

The secretarial course I choose at the college lasted two years and during this time Ivan had an apprenticeship as a builder in his father's business. At the weekend he would race Motocross bikes. This created more enthusiasm for me, as I did not know anyone else who did this and I thoroughly enjoyed the weekends when I would go with him to watch him race.

Ivan also had a car and he taught me to drive. Two months after my 17th birthday I was able to take my driving test. Unfortunately I did not pass, as I had developed a few bad habits. However, after a few private lessons with a qualified instructor within a month I had reapplied and passed. It felt like the world was really opening up to me. I applied for a job as a secretary for a haulage company in Armagh. When I got the job offer I immediately accepted. Just one dilemma the office was eighteen miles from my house in Glenanne and there was no bus route. I could drive, but had no car, and no money to buy one. But then Granny always said "Where there is a will, there is a way" I was willing to take the job but just had to find the way of getting there!

My mother took me to the bank and we explained that I had a job and needed to buy a car, and therefore I needed a loan. I borrowed £1,000 and thanked him a lot! There was no talk of what interest rate I would be paying, much less any negotiating of the terms. I was ignorant of all that and glad to get the money. We set out with this money that felt like a million to me.

We looked around a couple of garages to see what was available for my money. Finally we decided on a brown Mini. I was delighted, but as I was paying for this car, a brand new Mini Metro arrived in the showroom. The salesman told us that a girl was coming in later to collect it. I looked at every part of the shiny New Mini Metro and although I was delighted to have my own purchase, this Metro was the latest thing, the icon, the, car that was way out of my reach. As I drove my brown mini out of the forecourt feeling proud of myself for taking on the responsibility for the loan to buy this car, and also grateful for my mother and the bank manager in believing in me. I looked in the mirror at the big grin on my face, and in my head, I was saying "I am the owner of this beautiful car, thank you, thank you. This meant independence, I could drive off anywhere, I was free. I took one last admiring look at the Mini Metro car and promised myself one day I would buy myself a Mini Metro too!

Life seemed to be moving fast and I soon settled into my new job as secretary and of course taking my responsibility for my car and myself. I had to pay the loan back at £20 per week for three years, which was a total repayment of £3120. My wages were £80 per week, this was a huge portion of my salary, especially when you add all the running costs. There was not much left for luxuries or clothes.

After a year of working for this company there offices closed and I found myself looking for a new job. Fortunately I got one quickly for an engineering company who made farm machinery. Within a year of working in my new job I was able to change my car and this time the car I could afford was the dream Mini Metro. I now realised that if you focus on something you can make it happen. This was the start of me setting goals but at the age of eighteen I did not realise this.

At this point I was still going out with Ivan, and I suppose you could say we were growing up together. We never went on any foreign holidays but loved going to the beach nearby at Cranfield which is on the County Down coast about 40 miles from Glenanne. He would go into Kilkeel harbour and fish and I would walk on the beach and read books. He had his own hopes and dreams.

One day we went to this garage in Lisburn, near Belfast where we saw this beautiful Honda Prelude sports car going around on a turntable stand. The salesman stopped the turntable and Ivan started to examine the car. He pressed all the buttons on the dash, turned the steering wheel, switched on the engine to hear the sweet tone. We went for a test drive in another similar car and he took the brochure home with him, putting a tick at the colour of the outside of the car and the interior. Within weeks this would be Ivan's pride and joy - The dream car was to become his. Although no one had ever explained to us we could manifest our material dreams, we thought if you have enough ambition you could achieve anything you want.

CHAPTER 2

New Dreams & Beginnings

FAITH IN THE FAIRY TALE

Cinderella was always my real fairy story and I was sure that Ivan was my prince. When he asked me to marry him I said "Yes". It just felt like my dream had come true. I felt like he would put his strong arms around me, love and protect me for the rest of my life. Looking back now I really was naïve to think that by marrying Ivan my life was going to be wonderful and protected. My dream was that my husband, the builder, would find a building site, build me a castle, we would have children and live happy ever after in our little kingdom.

I had been Ivan's girlfriend for just over five years. We got engaged in March 1987. We decided not to have a long engagement, and so we married in October 1987. I was age 20 and Ivan was age 22. There was great excitement at my home as my three sisters and I threw ourselves into the preparations for the wedding. They were all bridesmaids as I was the first of my siblings to get married.

I had the Cinderella gown, a white long crinoline-style dress slightly off the shoulder, nipped in to show off my trim waist and wide skirts in satin and lace with a big satin bow on the back at the waist, with tails that went to the ground. The matching veil was three-quarter length trimmed in satin, attached to my headpiece which was a circle of tiny flower pearls, thicker to the front. My sisters wore purple taffeta dresses with big puff sleeves and wide skirts with a frill around the bottom. They had fresh flowers in their hair - white and yellow carnations and tiny little purple flowers. We were married in my family church and had our reception in a local hotel in Armagh about 20 miles away. It was a beautiful sunny autumn day and we were able to have many pictures taken outside. Our family and friends were all in attendance and in true Irish fashion, after our meal we partied, danced and sang into the small hours of the morning. It was one of the most special days of my life, and I was sad at how quickly the day had went by after seven months of preparation. The following day, Ivan and I flew to Majorca for our honeymoon. Where we relaxed and enjoyed the sunshine.

No one is responsible for anyone but themselves and there are things that you have to experience in order to grow and evolve. This was just the start of my life but in a simplistic way I could not think of anything other than a fairy tale of living happily ever after. I suppose that coming from a big family and being the minder of my other siblings, in a naive way I felt that I was getting my own life, finally not having to share with my other family members. The simple things, like cooking for two instead of eight felt intimate.

Building new dreams

We returned from our honeymoon a week later. Our new house was still to be built, on a site in a corner of a field that we had bought after we got engaged. This was just outside the town of Markethill in the countryside about seven miles from my family home and about five miles from Ivan's family. We had purchased a new mobile home and this was to be our temporary home until Ivan built our house. Ironic - married to a builder and no house!! The mobile home was cosy and big enough for the two of us. There were two bedrooms, bathroom, a galley kitchen, and a living/dining area. We had all we needed and it was cheap living, so we would save our money for our dream home.

Our plan was to live in the mobile home on my wages and save Ivan's. We would use this money to buy materials and on the weekends and evenings Ivan would build us a home. We also sold my car, the Mini Metro and had one car. I did not mind as the money was added to our house building fund and I liked driving Ivan's lovely sports car.

The first couple of months of married life flew by quickly as we were both working during the week and at the weekends we would drive around the countryside and look at houses. Soon we started to put our ideas and pictures of other peoples houses together to design our dream house. We then employed an architect to draw up our house - A beautiful 2500 square foot 2-storey house with a double-car garage attached to the side. Ivan measured it out on the site and we would have ample garden to the front and the back. Perfect!

Unexpected and Exciting news

We were only married about six months when Ivan came home from work one day and I told him to sit down as I had some news for him. I was going to have a baby! We were both a bit shaken and shocked as this was not the plan but if you want to make God laugh, you tell him your plans. After we chatted we decided that it could be worse; after the baby was born I could go back to work. A couple of weeks later I had more news for him. The one baby was now going to be twins!

Although the babies were due to be born on the 29th January 1989 they arrived on the 14th December 1988. A beautiful boy and girl weighing in at just 4lbs1oz and 4lbs2oz. I cried most of the day they were born, with relief that it was over and with joy that they were healthy. I kept looking at them in awe of their tiny yet perfect feet and hands, their little button noses and beautiful rosebud mouths. It was a wonderful and euphoric day. I felt that God had been so good to us by giving us a boy and girl.. How precious they were. I was overwhelmed by emotion and the feelings; we had made these incredible babies. I can remember thinking are they really mine; can I really take them home? They were so precious to us both from the moment they first arrived and nothing had prepared us for the love and joy we felt for these tiny bundles. They were the first grandchildren in my family, so there was great excitement and in Ivan's family, as he is a twin too. Both our son Graham and our daughter Lindsey had breathing problems. For this reason, and also because they were premature, they did not have the capability to suck and had to be tube-fed. However within a couple of days they were managing to get an ounce of milk into them before they were exhausted sucking. Our Christmas had definitely arrived early. Life was going to be very different. I suppose you could say we now had a purpose.

The permission for our house to be built arrived from the planning authority in early January and as we were busy with the babies it didn't seem to be a priority anymore. Life had taken on a new meaning. It was now a flurry of bottles and nappies; we were not sure which day of the week it was, never mind what time of the day. The twins were fed every three hours and it took just over an hour to feed each one.

Graham had a problem with the pyloric muscle in his stomach. When he was 6 weeks old it closed completely and he had to have an operation. On the morning of his operation we had left Lindsey with Ivan's sister and went to the hospital. I carried my dear little bundle of joy into the operating theatre, when he was sedated. I left in tears praying to God to watch over my precious baby. Ivan and I went out of the hospital for a couple of hours, and I remember us standing outside the hospital hugging and crying as we both prayed that God would look after our little boy and be by his side during the surgery.

When we returned, Graham had had his surgery, but had gone into a coma as he had breathing difficulties. I remember that night thinking I could not go home, but the nurse assured me that it was all right for me to leave, since I had only given birth to the twins six weeks prior, I needed my rest, and my other baby needed me also. Both Ivan and I left the hospital in a fragile state after going to the incubator and just putting our hands in and touching our little boy. I cried all the way home from the hospital which was about 50 miles, but when we picked Lindsey up and took her home I was delighted to find comfort in feeding her and holding her close. Thankfully, when I called the hospital the next morning Graham was more stable and starting to get well. We had a couple of very tough weeks with a baby in hospital and a baby at home. I had to dig deep and find the strength to keep going as my babies were my new world and I loved them dearly. I was always exhausted, as I would feed Lindsey at 7am and 11am, then leave her with Ivan's sister and arrive at the hospital in time to feed Graham at 3pm then again at 7pm. Then I would go home to feed Lindsey at 11pm and again at 3am and 7am. Driving 50 miles to the hospital and 50 miles home again was another challenge, but something or someone was giving me the courage and strength to persist and know that things could only get better. I was being shown how precious life is.

Building the dream

By the time the twins were just over 6 months old we decided that the mobile home was certainly not big enough for the four of us anymore and Ivan started to build the dream house. During the day, as I was still on maternity leave I would order the materials for the house and organise the deliveries. I was quickly learning the names of all the materials and making sure that all the ones Ivan needed were on site for him. In the evenings Ivan dug out the foundations and then started to build. From the kitchen window of our little mobile home as I washed up the dishes every morning I would look out over to our new home as it was materialising before my eyes.

This was a very different world to the one I was used to and it took a lot of readjustment. My old life had been getting up, showered dressed and out into the corporate world. Now it was feeding babies, changing nappies and giving love and nurture to my children. Although I loved them dearly, sometimes I was finding it all difficult. There was no adult conversation during the day to keep myself feeling stimulated I would take them out every day in their pram for a walk just to get out of the confined space. One day in particular, I recall the twins cried all day, and at about 3pm, as I could not get them settled, I put them in their cots and went outside and sat on the step and cried myself. What was my life about now? I had to focus and know that I had to be grateful for each block that Ivan laid down on these walls he was building. Each one was a block closer to our moving into our home. Ivan was getting tired now, but he too was persevering and using his knowledge and experience to encourage me that there would be an end to building this house. I think about halfway through and especially at later stages we were both losing faith and could just not see that one day it would all be completed and we could move in our house.

At night when I would put the twins to bed, I would go over to the house and look around at what Ivan had built. Now I could see where our kitchen, living room, sitting room etc, were going to be. Looking at the grey blocks, I would imagine what colour I would paint the walls, where I would place the furniture, and what it would be like to be living in all this space. When the roof went on, we celebrated: we were now able to see the complete picture. Soon the windows went in. When the plasterers arrived, there was a sense of exhilaration as we could now see the finish.

The twins were over 2years old when I went back to work, for a new company this time. My job was a managerial post, three days per week, challenging but stimulating. I welcomed the interaction with adults again and realised although I thoroughly enjoyed the time out with the babies, I had really missed some interaction on a daily basis with adults. It was giving me a renewed energy and something new to focus on. We were all getting tired with lack of space and the extra money would help with the cost of buying furniture for our new house.

Maybe it had taken us a little longer than planned as the twins arrived in the middle but now everything seemed to be coming together. We had our beautiful twins, who were just adorable and a true joy to us. When we were tired they would keep us entertained with chat, endless laughs and unique personalities. Through our persistence and determination every time we looked out the kitchen window of the mobile home we could see our dream materialising before our eyes it was worth the wait.

The time was coming close to moving into the house. I was getting really energized. I was choosing colours and fabrics for our home and at night when I came home from work and got the twins off to bed, Ivan and I would paint the walls of our lovely new home. Each weekend, I would make curtains.

On the 8th November 1991 we finally moved in. We had managed to stick to our plan of having no mortgage, and were so happy this long awaited day had arrived. It was thrilling to see the carpets being laid, our new furniture arriving, and the curtains going up. It was an extremely long and busy day. When we eventually got the twins off to bed in their new bedroom, we had a glass of wine to celebrate. We chatted and reflected on our journey so far. We had Ivan's lovely little sports car, our great jobs with reasonable salaries, and now a nanny to come into the house and mind the twins while we were working. Although we could not afford to decorate all the rooms we felt a real sense of achievement. We were relieved and happy that we had finished over half of the rooms and would get the others done at a later date. We knew it took more than a day to build the house and therefore it would just take a little more time to finalise the finishing touches but the most important thing was, we had not only dreamed our dream but we had made our dream a reality. I went to bed believing that my life could not get any better, it was just perfect, and everything I had ever wished for and more.

CHAPTER THREE

Near Death Experience

A couple of months after moving into our house we decided that we would take a much needed family break. So we went to the travel agents and booked to go away the last week in May and the first week of June to Majorca for our first family vacation together. We liked the island and it would not be too hot for the twins, who were now three years old.

We jetted off and had a much-needed break. In the morning we would stay at the hotel and the twins and I would swim in the pool. In the afternoon we would go to the beach or just lounge around the pool, catching some sun while the twins took a siesta in the shade. It was a very relaxing and enjoyable two weeks

Life-Changing Moments

A couple of weeks after we arrived home all tanned and relaxed I went off to work as normal and left the twins with Nanny. It was just a typically mad day at the office with phones ringing and the incessant demands. As I was preparing to leave the office, I called home, this was my usual pattern and said, "I'll be home in twenty minutes". As I put the phone down it started to rain, and as I was leaving the building a thunderstorm broke out

I ran to the car, threw my bag on the back seat, jumped into the driver's seat, started the car and drove out onto the main road. I had travelled about two miles when the rain started pounding down so heavily that the wipers could hardly clear the screen. As I rounded a corner, the car seemed to slide and then aquaplane across water on the road and headed straight for a tree. I frantically tried to brake, then steer, as I recalled Ivan telling me that if the car started sliding not to brake. But the car would not steer- it seemed as though the wheels were locked sideways. Frantically I continued to try to steer, as the tree was getting closer. Then, when I was about four feet from the tree, in a desperate attempt to save myself, I pressed my foot down really hard on the brake pedal and braced telling myself to "Hang on - it will be all over in a minute"

I never heard the "BANG." The tree was now in the middle of the bonnet and the car seemed to be hugging it. The floor was pushed down, the roof pushed up, the dash was broken around me, and the steering column was pushed up into my face.

Everything seemed to come in little snippets. All I can remember is someone sitting in the passenger seat saying, "IT'S OK - YOU'RE GOING TO BE OK." They seemed very shaken to me, and yet in my head I was saying I know I'm fine. The next thing I remember is someone at the driver's door with a crowbar trying to prise it open and thinking Oh no they are going to damage Ivan's lovely sports car. I recall saying to them "BE CAREFUL WITH THAT DOOR AND DON'T SCRAPE IT OR IVAN WILL KILL YOU". It seems like a ridiculous statement to make and so funny now as a scrape on the door was nothing to what I had just done to it.

Next, I was in an ambulance with an oxygen mask on my face on my way to hospital. I have no recollection of the fire brigade cutting me out or getting me into the ambulance. I remember the doctor in Accident and Emergency shining a light in my eyes and saying to his staff that he was worried about my head injuries.

I felt that I knew what was happening as the doctors and nurses were working around me and talking to me, telling me what they were doing. I had no idea of the extent of my injuries, nor do I recollect any pain at this time. I do however remember the nurse telling me that they would have to cut my dress off. Now I became agitated and told them that I had only bought it the weekend prior, and I would not allow them to cut it off. They laughed and joked and kept me talking to them, as I seemed to be drifting.

The Decision to Stay or Go

Suddenly it seemed as if I was coming out through the top of the crown of my head and I was floating up and up. Then I could see the nurses and doctors from behind and myself lying on the table. A wonderful sense of lightness came over me as I hovered above. The feeling was so calm and serene with the most beautiful sense of oneness as I drifted up and up towards the white light. There are really no words to describe this sense of oneness, love and light.

As I was travelling I saw Ivan come into the room and suddenly I thought of my children and the love I had for them. I thought I would just wait here a moment and see what Ivan has to say about his car. If he is cross, I will just go to this lovely calm and serene place.

As Ivan took my hand and said, "Don't worry about the car," I just seemed to slip back into my body and became aware of my body lying on the table again. Now I joke to Ivan and tell him, you never know the power of your word, because if you had said to me "what have you done to my beautiful sports car? I would have gone to the beautiful place filled with love and light and you would not have a wife anymore"

I still had no idea of the extent of my injuries or of what had actually happened. The doctor took Ivan into a room and told him that my right foot was broken; also the socket that fits the ankle into the foot had shattered like a bag of chips. He said he would have bolted and plated it, but there was nothing there to work with, it was smashed so badly. My left kneecap was broken and my pelvis was fractured on the right side. I had cracked two ribs and also my breastbone. The seat belt had burned one side of my neck and also down into my chest and around the pelvic area. The steering wheel had hit me in the face and detached the left side of my face. They had to stitch my left cheek back down unto the gum. Also my left cheekbone was damaged and my skull was fractured in two places.

In the middle of the night my body went into shock, and the nurse had to hold my tongue so that I would not swallow it. I was shaking all over and I just kept saying, "I nearly died, I nearly died." It was starting to sink in what had happened. For the next few days I kept trying to piece the bits together and work out what had happened, but I was not able to do so. I was confused and did not really know how I had got to the hospital or into the ward.

After a couple of weeks I was desperate to get out of the bed and return home, to the twins and start putting things in order. The twins were anxious - where had there mummy gone and what had happened to her? I was anxious to reassure them that I was fine.

When you are in a hospital bed for a few weeks, you learn that it is the little things that mean so much. Every day was a challenge and I had to rise to it. Every simple thing that I had taken for granted now all of a sudden presented a challenge that I had to overcome. I was so overwhelmed with gratitude when I managed to make it to the toilet and back on my own. The nurse said she had never seen anyone with such a big smile on her face. They told me I could go home if I could go to the bottom of the corridor and up the stairs on my crutches. I was ecstatic when I achieved this, although I had to go and lie down immediately with exhaustion as I was not allowed to put my right leg to the ground - it was in a heavy plaster from my thigh to my toes.

Finally after just over three weeks, I was allowed to go home. Even though I felt strong enough in the hospital when Ivan wheeled me out and the cold air hit me I felt so weak. When I arrived home, it all seemed strange. I could no longer get a drink for the twins, get them dressed or get down on the floor to play. My head was so sore and the strong painkillers I had to take were leaving me sleepy and unable to hold a simple conversation. In the middle of a sentence I would stop and have no idea what I had been saying. Also noise was a big issue for me. I could not have the twins shouting and playing around and the TV on. Even the TV and the cooker extractor fan on at the same time made my head so sore. All of our lives were turned upside-down in the couple of seconds it took from the car starting to slide to hitting the tree. Ivan now had to give up work for a while and look after not only the twins but also me. I needed help to get showered and dressed and could no longer do any of the household chores. All I could cope with was living minute-to-minute.

Be Thankful

From this experience I learned that you cannot take your life for granted. I was sure I would be home in twenty minutes.

I was grateful that I had survived and would see my children grow. I was grateful that there were people nearby that came upon me immediately after the accident, as I could have lain there on the roadside for a long time and perhaps have died.

Looking back now, I didn't realise how ill I was or really understand what had happened. It was like I was just going through the motions, its morning so I need to get up and it's night so I need to get to bed. There were so many injured parts of my body that I was in great pain from head to toe.

From my perfect life and what I thought were worries, such as what will I make for the dinner, and when will I be able to afford to get a room decorated. In a few seconds this life was taken from me, and I was living from minute to minute. I didn't even question how I would get back together. It seemed too difficult to try to put together and a plan. All I could do was live in a state of gratitude when I held my darling children. I was still here with them and grateful that my husband was there to care for us all.

CHAPTER FOUR

The Biggest Shock of All

Complete Devastation

We were all settling into our new routine and life was continuing to be a struggle for me. I was repeatedly playing the events of the accident over in my mind and trying desperately to piece them together but never seemed able to fill everything in.

I was home from hospital about three weeks when I remembered that I had missed a second period. The first time my period was due I was in hospital, just after the accident. I had spoken to the nurse and she told me not to worry it was probably the shock of the accident. However, one morning when I was in the bathroom I did a pregnancy test – I'm not sure why. To my shock it came up positive. I remember just staring at it and wondering what am I going to do? Shaken, I made my way around to the bedroom and lay down on the bed. When Ivan came in, I told him and we just looked at each other. I would have to call the doctor and see what he had to say.

When the doctor arrived at our home he told me that he would make an appointment with the gynaecologist at the hospital. He called him immediately from my house, and I was to go that afternoon. It was a Friday. My world was spinning too fast again and the shock of this was greater than the accident its self.

We got to the hospital at 4pm, and I recall sitting in the waiting room just staring in shock. I was brought into a room and the doctor asked me to get up on the bed, so he could scan my tummy. He confirmed the pregnancy but there was no heartbeat, my baby was dead. He said they would have to take me into hospital and take the foetus away. They would do this on Monday morning.

I got down of the bed in a daze and stared at the doctor in shock as he was writing the letter for me to bring to the hospital on Sunday. His voice seemed to be muffled, like the volume of the TV had been turned down. I took the letter and hobbled out on my crutches, stunned and in shock. Ivan said that we would not tell anyone, as we had enough to deal with and I agreed. We were both devastated and seemed to disconnect from each other in our attempt to deal with the pain in our own way.

When I got home I went to bed immediately and stared at the ceiling crying and wishing that I could die. I wished I could go to that lovely, bright, calm, serene, relaxing place. I fell asleep and awakened to the twins jumping over me telling me they loved me. How can children always know to say the right things? I was devastated but just smiled and hugged them.

The Time Had Come

Sunday eventually came, when we got to the hospital Ivan wheeled me in, in a wheelchair. I could not comprehend what was going on. The nurses looked at me with sympathy in their eyes but what could anyone say to make it better?

My leg was still in plaster from my toes to my thigh and my face was still badly swollen and bruised with one eye still closed. The burns and lacerations were still very visible down the side of my neck and chest. I am sure I was not a pretty sight.

We were shown to a private room at the end of the corridor away from anyone else. The doctor came in, and explained what he was going to do. After he left we both cried and Ivan hugged me. Then he said that he could not cope and needed to go home to the twins to be close to them. After he left, I just lay there staring up at the ceiling counting the holes in the pattern of the tiles, crying, wishing I could die, and wondering why no one was asking me if I was coping.

I told myself at that moment, I was a bad person. I desperately loved my children they were so important to me, yet I was now utterly devastated. I felt everything was my fault, I was angry with myself for the car accident. No one came to talk to me, and when it was time to eat they just brought my food into my room, set it down, and patted me on the hand. I could not stop crying I lay on the bed silently crying and yet inside I was screaming but there was no one to talk to.

The next morning I was changed into a theatre gown. Again I was crying but everyone just seemed to ignore it or told me I would be OK. When they wheeled me down the ward and stopped at the nurse's desk for my hospital notes, nurses touched my head, all with sympathetic faces, but no one spoke. The tears were flowing, I could not hold back. As I lay in the corridor of the operating theatre I wished I could get off the bed and run. When they wheeled me into the theatre and put the needle in my arm, I was sobbing uncontrollably and as the anaesthesia started to flow through my veins I sobbed into the darkness, feeling like a killer on death row. I truly wished that I would not waken but instead go to the beautiful light that would take all my pain away.

Dealing With The Agony

I came around again and soon was taken back to my room, where I spent the next three days on my own, crying. Ivan could not face coming to the hospital and found comfort in our children. This made me feel alone and disconnected from him. I needed him to be there, but it was just too much for him to bear. Finally on the fourth day the nurse said I could go home. No one at the hospital told me my feelings were normal. They never offered counselling. They just give me a letter for my doctor and discharged me. Ivan came to collect me, but this time as he drove us out of the hospital grounds, there was really nothing to say. I was not only physically broken but also mentally broken. I felt dead and numb inside. My soul was torn to pieces. I felt Ivan had no idea of the trauma I had been through over the past few days nor where my mind was and I could not seem to get the words to explain. I was back living minute-to-minute but worse, not wanting to live each minute.

When I got home, nothing prepared me for the intense mixed feelings I had when the twins jumped up on me to get hugged. The mental pain that ripped through my body was excruciating. The conflict between the love for my precious twins, and the hurt and anguish I felt for my baby that I had killed; by having the car accident was unbearable.

I could not comprehend the events of the traumatic days in the hospital. I could not speak as the pain was ripping and screaming through my body. I was afraid now that if I did talk to anyone I would just crumble and break. It was even painful to breathe. Somewhere deep inside I was angry, hurt and blamed myself. This little seed of hate and blame deep inside me was starting to grow.

At night, when I eventually got over to sleep, I would dream I had my baby in my arms. As I was wakening it would be slipping out of my arms then I would wake with a startle feeling like I had dropped the baby right out of my arms. It was gone leaving me feeling empty. Then I would realise that I was biting my lip so hard, it was bleeding, in an attempt to stop myself from screaming out in the small hours of the morning. Fear would overcome me and I was afraid to sleep again fearing I would repeat the nightmare. All I could do was sit up in bed feeling tortured by my feelings. Looking at Ivan sleeping and now wanting to blame him for not being with me or understanding how I was feeling. I was spiralling down into a big black hole and felt like I was never going to get out or recover.

Time to Forgive

From this I learned, that when emotions are high you stop taking in what anyone is explaining to you. Your thoughts and actions take over until you have no sense of reason and nothing is transparent anymore. Through no fault of your own you can lose your connection with your husband, your children and most of all yourself.

It took me ten years to work through my feelings with, counselling, reading self help books and meditation to finally realise that even if others try to make you understand that the incident was not your fault, until you forgive yourself you cannot move forward in life.

CHAPTER FIVE

Rehabilitation

By September, I was finally getting the plaster of my leg. I needed to be back walking again for my own sanity. I recall the day we went to the hospital to have the plaster removed from my leg. I had taken my shoes with me, a pair of white stiletto-heeled court shoes. No one had told me I would have to learn to walk again. In my ignorance I thought that they would just cut the plaster off my leg, I would put my shoes on, and walk out - Well, was I in for a shock!

When we arrived, the doctor took us into a small room and explained that he was really pleased with how my leg had healed. He then said in his opinion, as the ankle joint was so badly smashed that he felt I might be able to walk without a stick, but not without a limp for the rest of my life. He proceeded to say that the Achilles tendon had shortened on the back of my leg due to the way they had to position my foot to try to fix my ankle. I remember leaning slightly forward and saying to him "Excuse me, I don't do limps and I am most certainly not walking with a stick!" I put my hand up to stop his words from hitting me, I could feel the anger rise within me as I was refusing what he was saying. To me this would all be temporary, and I was not going to be like this the rest of my life. My head was whirling and going into overdrive. My thoughts were all over the place. What did he mean not being able to walk without a limp or a stick? I was determined that this would not be the case. He just looked at me and proceeded to say they would take the plaster off and I could then go to see the physiotherapist.

By the time the plaster was removed I was in a state of urgency to get to the physiotherapist. I also felt as if a red mist of anger was enveloping me. Ivan was not pushing the wheelchair fast enough for me and when I reached the physiotherapist I was almost crying with rage and anxiety. The first thing I said to him was, "What can I do to get rid of this limp?" He went through all the processes that I would have to undergo. He told me there were no guarantees, but he would get me walking, first with a stick and perhaps without a limp. I now had something to focus on, and this was not only good for me physically, but also food for my soul.

Therapy begins

It was no easy process I started by learning to walk in the hydro pool a couple of days a week and was really amazed when in the water it was difficult to walk, but on land as I called it, my leg felt like it was made of lead, really heavy and would not move at all. Every day I had exercises to do at home stretching my leg until I cried with the pain. After about six weeks, I felt like I was making no progress. I was still walking with two crutches and could not find the energy to give myself that extra push. I talked with the physiotherapist again, and he suggested that I start swimming. I would go to the swimming pool and force myself to swim 10 lengths; eventually I built it up to 30 lengths, three to four times a week. When I would get out, I was so exhausted it would take me at least 10 minutes to get to the changing room. Wrapping myself in a towel, I would go into the changing room and just lie down on the seat, crying with exhaustion. I told myself I could not do this anymore and not to be so hard on myself. Next I would say that I could do this, I would get through it, and remembered that my granny used to tell me to keep my chin up should my belly touch the ground. Every night, when going to bed, my right foot and ankle were swollen right up to my knee. In the morning, they were really stiff and sore and I had to push myself to get out of bed.

It was about the end of November, one day when the twins and I were at home; I went out to the kitchen on my walking sticks. I was determined that I was going to try to walk around the table. I let go of the sticks, held onto the table, and slowly pushed myself away. Then, with all my strength I took one-step forward, and then another, and another. Eventually I managed to get around the table and called to the twins to see what mummy could now do. My darling little three year olds stood watching as I pushed myself to walk around the table again and when I managed to make it back to them they were jumping up and down and shouting for joy, I was crying with relief I now knew that I would make it. I was so grateful just to be able to walk around the kitchen table, albeit with a dreadful limp but it didn't seem to matter. It meant so much to me. There was now hope.

Constant Struggles

I was still crying at least once a day. Life was still a struggle. When I would take the twins out to the shops to get our groceries. I would tell them to take my hand and that I could not talk to them until I stopped walking. In order to walk, I had to concentrate and tell myself to lift up my leg, bend my foot, swing my leg, put my foot back on the ground, etc. This was a big strain on me. Also, as we lived in the country, I had to face driving. I got behind the wheel and drove, again albeit very slowly, and if it rained - which it does a lot in Ireland - fear would overcome me. My hands would grip the wheel in panic that I would crash again, but somehow I managed to face my terror and overcome it. I realised that my challenges and weakness were quickly becoming my strength - That inner strength that I was unaware I had.

One day in my exhausted state, I remembered a book I had read some years earlier by an American lady called Louise L Hay. The book was entitled *You can heal your Life*. I went searching and found it, the story of this amazing inspirational woman was to be my lifeline. When I read it, I really understood her message of her life journey and how she healed herself from cancer. I decided that if Louise could do it, so could I. This little book was just what I needed at the time to help me move forward. I needed encouragement to persevere; I was determined that I would walk properly. Between the exercises and Louise's book I now had a focus. I would dig deep inside to find my courage, determined that I would persevere until I had reached my goal. I used little markers: for example if I could walk with out my stick at Christmas, I would get myself a new pair of shoes. Now the little light within me that was dim for so long was starting to glow again. I was coming back to life to fight for myself.

Destructive feelings

However, underneath all of this my inner feelings were being masked by my attempts to get myself walking. Deep down inside, I still felt like a killer, and hated and blamed myself for the accident and for wrecking my husband's lovely car. I was chronically depressed, physically wrecked, emotionally dead and struggling to even get out of bed every day with the pain. I could not think as far as the next hour. As a result, the relationship between Ivan and myself was getting very difficult. I felt as if he was "taking my children," as they continuously asked him to do things for them, like "Daddy, can you get me a drink of juice?" Of course, this was not Ivan's fault, it was because I was not able to do anything for them for so long that they were used to asking Daddy. Yet I felt angry and wanted to blame him. I hated him and blamed him for abandoning me at the hospital the time our baby died. To me, he had dropped me off at the hospital and walked out again not caring. After all, I was his wife and I needed him. I felt let down by him and had conflicting thoughts. If he really cared for me, would he have left the hospital? At this time I did not understand that everyone deals with their emotions in different ways, and now it seemed like he was taking my precious twins. We could not speak to each other - we constantly argued. I wanted to blame Ivan in the hope that it would make me feel better. I didn't do this intentionally. Inside I was drowning in my emotions and feelings, not sure who I was and what had happened to me.

CHAPTER SIX

Fairytale Break - Up

When my very foundation seems to have disappeared
When there seems to be a serious question about meeting my basic
needs of food and rent
When my future seems in terrible doubt and the world seems very
unfair
When my heart feels like its skipping beats and I have trouble
catching my breath
When it feels like I'm in shock and that someone has punched me
in the stomach
When it feels no longer safe to trust and there is temptation for me
to blame someone else for the predicament I am in
When I feel broken and fragmented, as if I were a jigsaw puzzle
that's been thrown in the air feeling that it's impossible to be put
back together again and feel normal again
When I have forgotten that the very essence of my being is love
and that I'm a strong spiritual being
I can be sure of one thing… it is not that God has abandoned me,
but I have abandoned God and I can choose once again
Let me always remember that I am one in God's presence, I rest in
God!

Desperate times and desperate measures

I seemed to bounce around for a couple of years in this semi-state of awareness caused strong painkillers, while trying desperately to put my life back in order. I was constantly exhausted and life in all was a huge strain. I had gone back to work and although it give me a sense of worth and routine it was too difficult. The pain was still piercing through my body daily. It was painful to just move around. I also had headaches and was exhausted from not sleeping, with nightmares of the crash and guilt. I felt as if I was not a proper wife to Ivan, and that I had let everyone down badly. Nothing could convince me any differently. Ivan and I just seemed to be screaming at each other at any chance. I felt so alone and there was no one to talk to. I desperately needed to feel loved by Ivan but all I could do was shout at him and find fault in everything he did. I was drowning emotionally, and the little girl inside of me was screaming. I could not take anymore. I needed space. I needed to breath and get at one with myself

On the 8th November 1994 when Ivan went off to work, I left the twins at school as usual; went back home and packed all my clothes, and some of the twins' clothes and their favourite toys. I sat down at the kitchen table and wrote a note to Ivan, telling him that I loved him dearly but I could not continue this life of constant shouting at each other. I was crying and my heart broke as I turned the key and locked the front door, of the beautiful dream home that we had made for each other, feeling as if I had just torn all our lives apart again.

I rented a town house in the local town of Markethill, just a couple of miles from our home. I had spoken to the owner just two weeks prior, viewed the property and made arrangements to move in. I needed space so I could breathe. My trust in everything was gone including in life itself. I was not sure where I would begin, but I needed the break to sort out who I was and what had happened to me.

At 2pm I collected the twins from school, I took them to the town house I had rented. We had juice, and I explained to them, in tears, that Daddy and I still loved them very much but as we were arguing all the time we just needed to be on our own for a while. They would live with me in this town house, and at the weekends they could go and live with Daddy. They were only five years old; I put my arms around them and felt guilt and anguish for ripping their world apart.

That night Ivan called me on the phone, as I had left my mobile number for him but no address. He told me to come home and not be silly, but I replied that I needed time and that he could come and get the twins at the weekend. That first night the twins and I slept together in a big king-sized bed. We all needed each other, and I felt guilty for taking them from their Daddy but hoped that our love for them would shine through.

When Ivan arrived for them at the weekend. I asked him in. I was crying, he was crying, and the twins were also crying. They were hugging us and in their innocence, trying to get us to hug each other with them in the middle in a hope to make everything all right. In that brief moment I realised that a block and a fear of rejection were building between Ivan and me and the lack of conversation between us over the past few years was now very apparent. We were very unsure of each other and being apart left us even more detached.

Eventually I got their bags together and Ivan left with them. I quietly closed the front door behind them, and as I heard the car moving off the driveway, I slid down the back of the door onto the floor, sobbing and crying. I felt so alone and desolate. After a couple of hours of non-stop crying and sobbing, I managed to come to my senses and pick myself off the floor. I went into the kitchen, took a large glass of water and a bottle of painkillers, and moved into the hall, climbed the stairs to the bedroom, and collapsed into bed. I stayed there from Saturday night until Sunday evening; every time I wakened I just took more tablets and went back to sleep crying. I stayed in bed until it was time for Ivan to bring the twins back again. Being on my own without the children was too much to bear. This was to be the routine for a number of months.

It took courage to pack up our belongings and leave, but I desperately felt I needed to do this so I would get stronger. Unfortunately, it seemed to be having the adverse effect. The nightmares were returning, and worse still, this time the nightmares were not only about the crash and my baby dying but now I was dreaming that rats were eating my feet. I frantically thrashed through the bed, screaming and wakening in a sweat to the deadly silence and being alone in the middle of the night.

These were my darkest days, when I really thought I was going to have a nervous breakdown. I could see no way forward and could not comprehend where I was going. Having had the courage to lift myself up out of the dark, my physical achievement seemed small in the light of the emotional turbulence inside me. The thought of going into the downward spiral again was almost too much to bear. How would I ever get out especially as I had not fully recovered from the accident. This time I felt it was the end. I would never recover, and some how I felt like it didn't really matter anymore. It felt as if I had been broken physically and managed to pick myself up, but now I was crumbling emotionally. I was sure I would break at any moment. I didn't know how strong I could be.

It didn't matter if family and friends were around me, I just felt so empty and alone.

It felt as if everyone had deserted me, but if I said that to anyone they would think that I was only feeling sorry for myself. Even though

I did not recognise it, I was now able to hold my feelings in from Sunday night until the following Saturday evening when the twins would leave. Then the crying would start again and my life would feel desolate and lonely, full of fear and anger.

One particular Saturday night after the twins had left, I was sitting on the stairs with my head in my hands just crying uncontrollably when I heard a knock at my door. I didn't answer, as I did not want to talk to anyone. I was angry; everyone had left me, including God. Yes, that was it - I was so bad that even God had left me. Then I heard something being dropped through my door, and I said out loud "Go away" as the tears streamed down my face. I wasn't worth caring about at all, and why would someone come to my door. After a while, curiosity got the better of me, and I went into the front hall and picked up this piece of paper. It was a tract from some church. I was angry and put it in the bin. The next day as I was emptying the rubbish, the same tract fell out of the bin. I picked it up and read "Footprints in the Sand" this was my message from God. He had not deserted me but was carrying me through the very dark days. I was not alone and he had been carrying me and giving me the strength to get through, it started to me to think of my journey so far and how grateful I was to be alive just after the accident. I placed the tract on my bedside locker and read it every night, it was comforting.

During the week I was going through the motions for the children, and at the weekend when Ivan had the twins, I retreated to my bedroom. I was angry at life and most of all disappointed in myself. In the solitude of my bedroom I was starting to read, I got out my Louise Hay Book the one I had carried around like a bible. I started reading through it and sometimes I would still be angry but as I read I was starting to find gratitude in my life again. I was grateful to be still in this life with my children, I was grateful for their love. Slowly I was registering where I was in my life and I started to write my feelings down and access myself.

Having spent a couple of weekend in my room reading, I decided that when Ivan took the children, I would stay up and cook myself a meal. What I realised was that I did not know what I liked to eat, drink, or do in this time that I had on my own. The food I had eaten prior to this was what the twins or Ivan liked. It was easier to ask everyone else what they wanted and just make their preference. I was happy to eat anything. This date with myself was somewhat challenging. I was astonished to realise that I did not really know myself. For all my life to this date, I had made decisions to help others. I was now realising that the person I had neglected most in my life was myself. This was the start of my challenge to uncover and rediscover who I was and to love myself and celebrate myself in a quiet way. It is difficult for us to see how unique and special we are. Deep down inside I knew I was a survivor. I had the ability to overlook other people's pity and raise myself above all the suffering. I needed to get back the zest for life I had when I was a little girl - feel my fear and do it anyhow.

The weeks sped past and the twins were off school it was June 1995, the weather was exceptional - a real heat wave hit Ireland. It was just what I needed - some time with the children and some sun. We had a very lazy summer. I bought a table and chairs for our patio, and we ate out there most days. The twins had a paddle pool that we would fill every morning. As the sun rose it would warm the water, and after lunch they would play around in the pool and I would lie back in the sunlounger and relax before making a barbeque tea. It was a beautiful summer and I was starting to relax. I had fewer nightmares and I began to be at one with myself. On the weekends I would now go for a walk in the park beside our house or drive down the Co. Down coast to Cranfield about 40 miles, to the beach and have a walk along the edge of the sea where the sound of the waves gently breaking onto the sand seemed to calm my soul. The little girl inside of me was not screaming anymore and I was getting at one with myself. I was starting to realise that suffering and pain are relative but they also unite your body and soul.

So Many Choices

By the end of the summer, Ivan and I were starting to communicate better with each other, he would come up on the odd day when we were sitting in the sun and have some tea with us. We would make small chat and started to feel relaxed around each other. Then he started to press me about coming back home. I could feel the fear rise in me and would not answer. He asked me one day if at the weekend I would go with him and the twins down to our house. I agreed but by Friday could feel myself being really frightened, and as the hour approached I could not go. It was just too much for me. I was just getting to be comfortable with myself and was not sure if I was strong enough to make a big change again.

When Ivan came to collect us he could see by my face that I would not be going. He tentatively asked me where my bag was and I could see the disappointment in his face when I told him I could not go. But in an attempt to help him feel better I told him that if he came back for me the next day, I would go and have dinner with him and the twins at our home.

That night, as I lay alone in bed, the nightmares came again. I realised that I was very fragile, but I could not let this take over my life. Would my fear of it all going wrong again stop me from going back home and having us all together as a family. I didn't know if I had the strength or the courage to go through this again. I prayed to God to give me strength to make the right decisions. When Ivan called to collect me, it felt very strange to be in his car, and when I got to what used to be my beautiful home I felt like a stranger in it and very uncomfortable. I managed to eat dinner with everyone, and then we went for a drive and took the twins to the park. This seemed to make Ivan really happy and the twins were delighted that we were all together again. After a couple of weekends like this, I eventually stayed over a night and then Ivan was desperately looking me to come home.

The twin's seventh birthday was approaching fast, and also Christmas. Ivan was now really putting pressure on me to return home for both occasions. I was not sure, as I felt we had not resolved things between us. I really think that I feared making the decision because I doubted I would have the courage to leave if it did not work out. I was in turmoil once more.

I had to weigh up the situation. The twins needed to have their mummy and daddy together again. It was more secure for them, and I felt I owed them that much. I knew Ivan still loved me. My fear was growing I felt like a rabbit caught in the headlights! What was my fear? Was it really that my mirage would go wrong again or was it that still, I was searching to come to peace with myself? or maybe it was that I did not love myself? It is difficult to try to make good a relationship that has gone bad, and most relationships never do make it back together again. I had to consider that Ivan had understood, and his patience and loyalty to me were wonderful. I had to admire his loyalty to me. I knew deep in my heart that I too wanted us back as a family again… It was only my fears holding me back!.

LIGHTNING STRIKES TWICE

One Sunday morning the twins and I were returning from staying with Ivan the night before. I was driving into town and I drove onto a roundabout. As I passed the next junction on the roundabout, a car came out too fast and hit the side of my car, sending us sideways across the road. We hit the kerb so hard that the wheel broke from the axle. I was stunned for a second and did not know what had happened. Looking into the back of the car, the twins, who were six years old, were still in their car seats but there faces were bleeding. Luckily, they had only superficial cuts from the glass of the broken side window. I was finding difficultly in breathing as the seat belt had caught my chest again. An ambulance arrived and I needed oxygen. We were all taken to hospital to be checked over luckily all the injuries were minor we were discharged that evening. When Ivan arrived at the hospital, I felt this overwhelming urge that I needed him. I needed all of us to go home all of us together.

Together Again

That evening after the accident, when Ivan left the twins and me, I knew I needed to make my decision about us getting back together. Had this accident been God's way of telling me to go home. Had I not been listening to the small and subtle hints? In a couple of days I give Ivan my news. I took a huge leap of faith and told him I would go home and before I had time to really think about it we were all back together again two days before the twins seventh birthday and Christmas 1995. The twins seemed really happy but I felt like a stranger in my own home. Ivan actually felt afraid to go to work in case I would move out again while he was gone. It was evident that we would have to work on our relationship. However, one thing we knew for sure. The children were happy and feeling more confidant and secure. After all we were the two most important people in their lives; we were their creators. As we both started to relax and enjoy being together with the children we loved dearly the love and respect we had for each other started to grow.

CHAPTER SEVEN

Becoming a Family Again

Connection with my husband

After a few months together again as a family, I started to feel more secure. Ivan and I were now able to communicate on a deeper level. It was comforting in the night to have someone to cuddle up to and to feel his strong arms around me. We were talking now more than ever and realising that it was lack of communication that made everything go wrong. We had each been through a traumatic time and were coming to a better understanding of each other as well as a deeper mutual respect. We both realised that everyone is an individual and entitled to make their own decisions about life and situations. I came to accept that it was all right that Ivan left me at the hospital at the time when our baby had died, because that was his way of dealing with the situation. Just because he didn't sit and hold my hand didn't mean he wasn't hurting. He was hurting deeply and I had to understand this. Also, he had to understand that because he didn't stay at the hospital I felt rejected and unloved by him. I was his wife and needed him, and felt let down. This left me detached from him. We had lost connection, and as the gap widened, I felt there was no return and this caused me to leave him.

I also realised that in order for me to feel loved by Ivan and be whole and complete, I would have to live a true life and no longer pretend to be anyone but myself. By this I mean that as a wife and a mother you tend to make decisions based on how it benefits everyone else and not how it personally impacts you. In other words, it is sometimes easier to hurt yourself by saying nothing than to hurt others. This is not easy, especially as my character is to be a minder. Similarly, the car accident and the entire trauma related to it contributed to my loss of identity. I became depressed, despairing and fearful. But I had evolved and would continue to do so, to search my soul and to love each part of myself until my soul and body would unite and I became whole.

For me personally, the most difficult part was still the pregnancy and our baby dying, I felt like a killer. Although we could now talk about it, I would whisper as if it was something that was painful to get out. It was clearly evident that I could still not forgive myself.

To get through a new challenge in my life, my initial tactic is to distract myself until I can deal with it. True to my character, this time I choose to redecorate our home and make it better than it ever was. This was January 1996 a new year and a new life. It was important to change the look of all the rooms in order to manifest a new start. The twins were now six years old and we made special little bedrooms for them. We also redecorated our own bedroom and our sitting room and put granite worktops in the kitchen. Making our home different was like putting our lives back together in a visual way. In our relaxed state, our creativity flowed as we transformed our home for our new journey in life. We started to feel comfortable, and enjoyed our family life as I slowly let go and became at one with myself.

Birthday Distress

By late 1997, almost a year from the twins and I returning home, I had been having a few minor problem and was attending the gynaecologist. A few days before my 30th Birthday, I had an appointment at the hospital for a check-up. When I got into the examination room with the doctor she asked me how I was feeling and a few other questions. Then she drew a line on a piece of paper and started to draw an arrow going through the line. As she drew, she said the results of your smear test shows that the cells have gone beyond this point, which is 'borderline'. "We propose to do a hysterectomy in four days". She proceeded to explain, "We have got two problems. One, if you don't have a hysterectomy the cancerous cells will spread through your body. Two, whenever we perform a complete hysterectomy you will go into the menopause and will have to take Hormone Replacement Therapy. As you are 29 years old, we cannot guarantee after 10 years you will not get breast cancer". Then she said " Would you like to bring your husband in for me to speak with?" to which I replied, "He is at work. I am here alone"

Again I sat there dumbfounded. The doctor repeated that they would perform the surgery in four days, which would be on 30th birthday. I asked her if I could call her in the morning. I just needed out, time to think and come to terms with what she had just told me. I left the hospital with my stomach churning. I felt like I was going to be sick and my head was pounding. When I got to the car, I started the engine, but I could hardly get it in gear for my legs were shaking. I was not even sure of the way home.

When I arrived at my sister-in-laws, to collect the twins, she saw that I was distressed and told me to lie down. As I lay in her bedroom I realised again, for the second time in my life, that my children needed their mummy. Even if I only had 10 years, I'd be happy. It was another chance to have more time with my children. I agreed to have the operation. That night as I lay in bed, this time I thanked

God for having a problem that could be sorted out and promised him that if he would give me the 10 years, I would live my life to the full. I knew it would not be an easy journey, but I also knew that, as in the past, now was only a dip in my life. I had a choice. I could become a victim of what had and what was happening to me, or I could rise above it all. I promised myself I would rise. As I drifted off to sleep, anxious about going into hospital in the next few days, deep down inside I just knew that I would make it.

Hospital Anxiety

I was really nervous going into the hospital to have the operation, as this was the same hospital and the same ward where I had came when my baby died. As I took the lift I could feel my legs shaking and when the doors opened the clinical smell of disinfectant hit me in the face. I thought I was going to be sick. This time I was shown to an open ward with three other women already there. It was welcoming to have company, and the staff were very thorough in explaining all the procedures as I settled in to have all the tests needed prior to major surgery.

On the day of the operation, I was trying to be brave. Ivan was trying to be more supportive this time, as he knew I felt he had walked out on me the last time. He came to see me that morning. Strangely I realised how far I'd come because it was me now telling him to go home before the nurses came to take me for the surgery. This time I didn't want him to be there. I realised IT DOES NOT MATTER HOW LONG SOMEONE STAYS WITH YOU. THERE ARE THINGS IN LIFE THAT YOU MUST DO ON YOUR OWN. He could have held my hand all the way to the theatre door, but I still had to go into theatre, hold out my arm and have the anaesthetist put me to sleep. It was my body that had to be operated on. At this time I had a revelation. I realized that it was wrong that I had blamed him for leaving me. I now knew that he couldn't have stayed with me.

I was now in the process of literally reliving that earlier experience that I had replayed to myself for so many years.

This time as I was wheeled to theatre, I was calm and thanked God for the gift of my life. After the hysterectomy was performed and I came to, although I was in a lot of pain, but I was grateful that it was all over and that I was on the road to recovery. The operation took a lot out of me, and that night when Ivan came to see me I only vaguely remember him being there. As he was leaving, he bent down and kissed me on the top of the head. I recall smiling.

Just after he left, I had this distinct smell of my late grandmother's perfume, and as I was drifting in this state of semi-consciousness, I opened my eyes to see her sitting at the bottom of my bed smiling at me. She said, "Roslyn, I am here with you watching over you. You're going to be fine… Keep your chin up" and then she left. I drifted off knowing that I was safe and all would be well. For many years I never talked about my grandmother's visit as I thought people would be sceptical, but I know for sure that she was there that night when I needed reassurance. I can call upon her anytime, and she is always there with me to comfort me.

Although I was drugged up with morphine to help ease the pain, this time it was only physical pain and I knew it would pass in time. It was a few days before they stopped the intravenous morphine but then the doctor realised that I needed four units of blood. When they started to administer the blood, I ran a really high temperature and rejected the blood. This meant that I had an infection, and so I had to have antibiotics intravenously. As I had just had my ovaries removed, I had no hormones and spent a whole day crying. This time it was explained to me that it was normal, when you have no hormones and they would start my HRT immediately. Soon I started to feel better and the blood made me stronger. When I was able to get out of bed and go the toilet on my own, I was so grateful, as I had been at other similar times in my life. The little things we take for granted mean so much to you at such times.

As I lay in the hospital bed, I remembered a piece in Louise Hay's book that if you do not forgive yourself the pain lodges itself in that part of your body and creates dis-ease. This dis-ease, if not let go of, will manifest itself into DISEASE and eventually that part of you will give up and die. Is what I had done to myself? It was now time to take control of my life.

The Dream

One day I had been drifting in and out of sleep and having a recurring dream. Not just any dream, this was my dream. I could not wait for Ivan to come to the hospital. When he arrived I started to tell him my dream and how I was going to make it a reality. I was going to buy a shop and open a ladies' boutique, in Markethill, the town where the twins went to school. I was so excited I almost of jumped off the bed. Every time I closed my eyes, the dream would come and take over my mind, becoming more vivid each time. As I lay in the hospital bed I didn't even think about the "how". I just knew I would have this shop and live this dream.

I arrived home from hospital ten days before Christmas; by the time I got home I was totally exhausted and had to go to bed straight away. I was also in great pain. I stayed in bed during the day, and just after tea each evening Ivan would carry me down the stairs to the sitting room, where I would sit for a little while with the twins until the pain overcame me and he had to carry me back to bed. I managed to stay up the whole day of Christmas Day but on Boxing Day I could not get up at all. It was evident that I had pushed myself too hard, and if I was to get well I had to look after myself better.

Somewhere deep down inside I ached to get out of bed and get to work on this new dream that was spinning around in my head. It was becoming so real that I was almost sure that if I drove up to the town, the shop would be there. It was totally taking over and all the reasons to start this little venture were positive:- My mother had worked in fashion most of her life and I had a good understanding of it from a child, my back ground in booking keeping and management give me the skills necessary to run a business and just to make it perfect the twins went to school in Markethill and therefore they would be able to come to me after school. Ivan was not as sure as I was; something deep inside told me this was the new part of my journey. My gut instincts were screaming, "Yes, yes" to this and I could not wait to get going.

As the days went past and I regained my strength. The bubble of excitement was rising from my very core. I felt so alive as everyday I was still dreaming my dream of the boutique. Towards the end of January 1998 I talked to a girl on the phone that had a shop to let, however she had since decided to open a flower shop in it. I wished her well and asked her if she knew of any other shops. She told me about a gentleman who was talking about retiring. Within a couple of days I had got myself together and driven up to Markethill to make myself known to him. He was very polite but not sure if he really wanted to retire or not. I asked him if he were to retire what price would he be looking for his shop? A couple of weeks after that I invited him to my house for lunch. We agreed on a price and that he would vacate at the end of July so I could prepare to open the shop at the beginning of the autumn/winter season in September.

I had never felt so alive in all my life. Everything was falling into place and it felt totally right for me. Not only was it good that I could have my own business and be the person I wanted to be but also the twins could come to the shop after school and be with me. This was the cherry on top of the icing on the cake. It was perfect. I thanked God for the opportunity to express myself and help others.

Reaching out to help others would give me the opportunity to connect and grow.

Chapter Eight

The Ladies' Boutique

By February 1997, everything was starting to move fast. I quickly learned that if this shop was to open in September I would have to take myself to the fashion fairs in February. These were in London, Dusseldorf and Paris.

Fashion Fairs

I managed to get to London and Dusseldorf in Germany to buy my first season's clothes. This was three months after having the hysterectomy. I was still getting used to taking HRT and I was feeling unwell, but I was thrilled to be doing something completely different from anything I had ever done before. This was a new challenge and I was rising up to it.

I flew to London, and on the way into the city on the train, rang Ivan to see if all was fine with him and the twins at home. I then went on to say that I was feeling tired and unwell and felt like crying. I then asked, "Why am I doing this?" to which Ivan replied, "I don't know, but you're the one that wants this." It was not that Ivan didn't want me to have the boutique but as he loved me his fear of me failing was what made him nervous. I laughed and hung up the phone. He was right, I was the one that wanted this and I had to focus, as this was my dream and I was making it real.

Visiting the fashion houses and fairs, all the samples were in a size 10, I quickly grasped that you had to look at the design and structure of the garment and imagine what it would look like in a size 16, 18 or 20. As the shop was to stock sizes from 10 to 20, not all the labels would suit bigger sizes. It was hard and exhausting work, like a mega-shopping trip. All the fairs and shows were set up like collections of little shops, each having its own specific label. I really enjoyed them, although they were both mentally and physically exhausting as you were constantly making up outfits, looking at structure, deciding colours and making it all fit your budget.

Like everything in life when you think you have it all sussed, you get the odd little surprise that seems to knock you down, if you let it. My surprise came when I approached the bank to borrow the money to buy the shop. I never envisaged a problem and therefore never tried to sort this out until early March after I had the buying trip over.

I had made an appointment, and prior to arrival had gone over all the scenarios in my head. I had my business suit on and arrived on time. They showed me into the boardroom, where two managers were sitting. I told them my story of how I wanted the money to purchase the building, to create my shop. To which they replied that I had no experience in this field and I was too high a risk. I sat back in the chair and looked them both in the eyes. I explained that we had been banking with them for many years and that our house had no mortgage and was worth a lot more than the shop - to which they replied I still had no experience and therefore they were not interested. Well, after everything I had been through in my life, I was not going to let this get to me. So I smiled at them and said that I was really sorry that they were going to miss out on a really good business. I shook there hands and left. This was not the end of the world, or even a problem; it was only a situation. I was going to be opening this shop I was determined I would find someone to lend me the money. After being turned down by another two banks. I was even more determined I would get this money. My grandmother always said where there is a will there is a way. I would just have to be imaginative, after all I believed in this dream and knew it would be successful. It came to me like a bolt of lightening. I would mortgage my own home, sure I was just buying another asset that would add to the value of what I already had. I convinced Ivan that it would be fine to do this as my plan B would be if the boutique did not work out I could rent the shop and cover the loan this way. Within a few days of taking this approach I had the money.

The summer months were taken up with the final purchase of the premises. Ivan took time out from working for his father to do all the refurbishment. I had told him it was just a "Small job" and he could do it no bother. In actual fact, he had to replace the floors, walls and ceilings, rewire the entire building, and put in a heating system and a new shop front. So I guess you could say I just bought the site!

I revelled in designing all the décor down to the fine details. As there was no other Boutique in Markethill, it was important to me that this was not just going to be any Boutique it was going to be an experience.

Finally on the 18th September 1997 "Lady R" was born.

From the moment you pushed the brass "R" door handle (which I got specially made) stepped onto the luxurious wool carpet, and heard the soothing background music, you knew that you could unwind and give yourself time.

I added little touches such as a play area for kids and a comfy couch for husbands to relax on at the back of the shop near the changing area. The changing rooms were spacious with enough room for a chair, and with the personal touches of tissues and body spray. The clothes were all displayed along the walls, creating an open feel throughout the shop, with little displays dotted throughout. The price of the designs was mid-market but to me it was not about money. It was about making women feel good about themselves. I wanted to help them create a new image for themselves to experiment with styles they might not have chosen and give them different looks and make them comfortable in who they were. I especially liked putting together a complete ensemble for a more formal occasion like a wedding or ball. The ranges went from a size 10 –20 and the styles were from casual to wedding/formal wear as well as jewellery, hats, handbags and accessories.

Opening day was a great success, with a wine and cheese, and a local professional model showed off some of the fashions. Everyone was made very welcome. I always felt it was important to make people feel welcome and at ease. When the shop opened I had one girl to work with me and as it became busier I expanded to three staff. They were all trained to welcome the customers, stand back and let them browse. If the customer needed some help, they were to discreetly be there to give them guidance in choosing styles that best suited not only their body shape as well as their lifestyle. It was important to me that everyone loved and enjoyed the clothes that they bought. As it was also important when I was buying that I found clothes of luxurious quality and beautifully cut cloth for the money.

I spent the first couple of months watching. I observed, where people looked first in the shop and how receptive they were to different styles. I chatted to and learned from both my staff and customers. My confidence was growing and I was overwhelmed to think that my dream was now a reality and women loved it. The boutique, give me a real sense of purpose. I was now connecting with other women. Some of them would confide their problems to me and I would listen with empathy. I knew pain when I saw it, and I always tried to make them feel better. I tried to get them to look at their situation in perhaps a different light and have them leave feeling that they were not alone. By reaching out to these women and drawing from my own experiences in life, I had the opportunity to give back.

Soon I came to realise that if I hired an image consultant to train my staff and me, then we could give even more to our clients. This was amazing. I learned so much about how styles suit body shapes, and which colours suit your hair and skin tones. It was really useful and we were soon giving the customer the benefits of our training.

On the Catwalk

It was important for me to give back in the community, as I had my business in Markethill town and only lived out of town about 3 miles in the country. I did this by hosting two fashion shows a season for local charities. It was again hard work but fun. I had a wonderful team of girls who would model for me, spanning different age groups, and another invaluable couple of girls who worked behind the scenes ensuring that the girls got dressed properly and also that the clothes all got back on the appropriate hangers.

For the first couple of shows I would help in the background and then go and watch the girls strut their stuff down the catwalk. One night as I listened to the compere read from the notes that I had written for her, I realised that although she was a professional, I would be able to do this much better myself, as I could also give extra fashion tips.

When the time came for the next fashion show I had set myself a new challenge, I would have to move outside my comfort zone. I picked out a beautiful ball gown and when the show started I was welcomed on stage to compere myself I realised how my knowledge of the fashion not only made the show more interesting but also give the women new ideas and fashion tips to make their existing wardrobe look good or if they had a special occasion next year I could tell them the fashion colours as the buying of the clothes was almost a year in advance. It also helped me to build a bond with the perspective customers.

At the end of the night I was asked to walk to the end of the catwalk in my gown. This became the pattern of shows to come. Every time I bought for the next season, I would choose a beautiful piece for myself especially for these shows.

At the beginning and the end of each season I would do a mail shot and invite all my customers on a specific night and host either a New Season Preview or a Sale Preview with wine and nibbles. These were real social events. Many looked forward to these special nights, when they could chat with other women and make new friends as well as check out the latest fashion trends or pick up a bargain.

News of the Lady R experience spread fast and soon it became a good business. Our range had now expanded to mother of the bride/groom outfits, wedding wear to ball gowns. We still stocked special occasion for guests and casual weekend wear. Hats, handbags, costume jewellery and shoes. It gave me great pleasure helping women and seeing them transformed in fashions they might not of considered. As their confidence in me and my staff grew, so did my self confidence. I really felt like life had a sense of purpose. I felt alive.

Containing the "Mummy Gilt"

On the personal side it was great to have my children there with me. They were age 9 when I opened the shop and although they were acting more grown-up some days when I would leave them at school and they were feeling vulnerable, as I let them out of the car I would place a little kiss right in the palm of their hand. Then I would close there hand tight and tell them that it would stay there all day just for them, and if they felt sad, that all they had to do was hold there hand up to there mouth and get mummy's kiss. Then I would remind them that I was just up the street and soon it would be time for them to either walk to the shop or I would go and collect them. It was comforting for them and for me to know that we were so close.

When they arrived at the shop from school we would have a cup of coffee or juice and I would chat to them about their day. They would then go and do their homework in the little studio Ivan had made for us upstairs. It was an open-plan room containing a kitchen and breakfast bar, a corner workstation for me to do some paperwork, my filing cabinet, and a little couch for the twins to relax on. I felt I had the pleasure of both worlds - of being a businesswoman and a mummy - and so the feeling of mummy guilt left me.

I always say that when Mummy is in business, so are your children. The shop was good for the twins, as they learned how to speak with adults and interact in a respectful and appropriate manner. They learned how to answer the telephone in the right manner and send a fax, and when we were stock taking they loved to join in the counting or ticking off the stock. Lindsey especially loved unpacking the new stock and hanging it up, and her delight on a Friday was to tidy the jewellery cabinet. At night when we were ready to go home, they loved to cash up the till. They were unwittingly learning skills that would be of great use to them in later life, skills that quickly became second nature to them and raised their business acumen to a high level.

Time Out for Me

I had opened Lady R in September 1997 and by Christmas 2003, after almost seven years of running this business I realised that I had given it my all and needed time out for me. I was having great difficulty with my back and feeling really exhausted. I spent my only day off, Sunday, washing, cleaning and cooking before the work to started all over again.

In February 2003 my dad was diagnosed with cancer and by Sept 2003 he was very ill and as we are a big family, we all offered our support to our parents. We made a little timetable that suited each of us at specific times through out the day to be there to comfort and support.

For a short while life would be different, everyday at lunchtime I would leave the shop and take time out to nurse my Dad. One afternoon as I sat with him, I realised that it did not matter how long or how hard I held his hand. He was dying and would be gone soon, and there was nothing I could do about it. Within six weeks he had passed away, and like we all do when we suffer loss, pain and grief we question ourselves as to what we are doing with our lives.

This prompted me to have a good look at what I wanted from life at this point. I was grateful for everything but like all our lives there are times that you have to sit back, access where you are and make a decision on what is best for not only you but also your family. I had to be selfish for us as a family. I had given Lady R my all and now it was time to look closer. Markets were changing as to how people were buying clothes, big fashion outlets were opening in the local major towns Newry and Portadown that I could not compete with and now cheaper clothes were no longer bad quality.

On the personal side I decided I wanted time out to be with the twins. They were 15 years old and I wanted to be able to support them through their last couple of years in high school, when they would be doing their GCSE exams. It was important to me to share the last couple of years of their childhood. I had managed to repay the mortgage I had taken out on my house to buy the shop. My back was causing great distress, and the medics were looking to perform back surgery, with less than a 60% chance of recovery. I decided this time that before I would do any more damage to myself; I would listen to my body and give myself time out with the children, and most of all a little time for myself.

I finally reached my decision over the Christmas holidays 2003. It was an agonizing one – to close the shop. Personally it made me feel sad as by closing "Lady R" felt like I was killing a part of me. I had created this place and now I was stopping or closing it but I thanked God for the opportunity to touch others, to give back in my local community. I realised that in creating this shop I had made myself a unique opportunity; its importance in my life was that it had helped me feel fulfilled by helping others.

I always think it took more courage for me to stand up and say that I was going to close the shop than when I announced I would open it. I felt I was letting both my customers and staff down but sometimes in life you have to look at what is affecting you personally. I had made my mind up, had my plan and knew that this would be for the best. I also knew by closing "Lady R" that I could rent the premises to someone else to allow them to create something unique to them and live their dream.

Sometimes society tries to make you feel like you have failed or the fear of letting people down stops you from moving forward with what is right for you. It is equally important in life to realise when you have had enough, when something you do no longer serves the same purpose or makes you feel alive. I was tired, my body needed a new challenge but first I needed some rest.

On 28 February 2004, the closing day, my loyal customers called in to wish me well. As I let my staff out the door I took one look around and thanked God for this opportunity of the wonderful business I had, for the staff and customers.

With one last glance I stepped out into the Main Street leaving a part of me behind but this time I knew that it had been a wonderful experience, my feminine energy was resorted as well as my confidence and business sense. I had grown and learned many things over the 7 years. I would move forward with a new identity and more confidence from this experience, from this little spark of imagination when I was lying in the hospital bed I had created and grown this business, that had helped mould me into the woman I am today.

CHAPTER NINE

Property Portfolio

Planning the Future

Two months after opening the shop, I felt that fashion was a fickle business, but I wanted to have this little business for as long as my twins were in school. To ensure this would happen, I felt I would need to back it up with something else, some other enterprise that would not take up all my time, as a shop was demanding. Finally I decided that I would buy a little house and rent it out.

I was aged 30 at this time and I had a new plan. Ivan was still working in his fathers business and I looked at this as an opportunity to build security for my family, also as I was not sure how long I would be able to work with my back and leg still giving me some difficulties. My goal was to have one million pounds in property by the time I was 40years old. This would be my private pension plan, hopefully in the ten years, some of the properties would have their loans paid off and some would have grown in value and I would be able to retire if I wanted to.

I looked around locally and saw that I could buy a two-bedroom street house in Portadown for around £20,000 and that the rental income on it would cover the mortgage. This made good business sense to me, and the town was easily accessible from my house. I found one that suited the budget and placed a bid, £20,000 on it.

I remember the telephone ringing in the shop. I was tidying underneath the counter. When I picked up the phone a gentleman asked for me and said that he was pleased to tell me that my bid had been accepted. I put the phone back on the hook and put my head down for a minute wondering what had I just done. Then I could hear the twins saying, "Mummy who was that on the phone". I looked up and there they were, looking over the top of the counter with an inquisitive expression on their faces, as 9 year olds do. To which I replied, "Oh God! I just bought a street house, your daddy is going to kill me"

I had very little money and just the cash flow of my business. I had to think of how I could get this financed. I asked a bank manager I know out to lunch. At the previous company I worked for, we used to have a joke and said that if the bank manager paid for your lunch you would get the loan. Over lunch I explained to him what I was looking to do, and he seemed interested and impressed. After we finished our lunch I asked the waitress for the bill, but the bank manager said, "It's fine Roslyn, I will pay". I could relax, as I knew what he would say next. He asked me when it would be convenient for me to come into the bank to sort out a loan offer. It took me three days to get the loan offer and three days for me to summon up the courage to tell Ivan I had bought this house. It was not that I was hiding anything. I was afraid that Ivan's fear would add to my own and it would make me challenge and doubt myself and stop me from moving forward with the plan.

One Down, Many to Go

When I finally got the keys and we arrived at the house, Ivan seemed somewhat amused as he looked around. He then said to me, "How do you plan to rent this house?" I could feel myself getting irritable. I replied "Simple!" and took an envelope out of my bag and wrote on the back of it TO RENT and my mobile number. I then placed it carefully in the corner of the window at the front of the house. The next day someone rang me, and when I showed the family the house, they wanted it and moved in immediately. They were wonderful tenants. They even decorated and kept the house in good condition. I only sold this house a couple of years ago with the tenants still there.

By the end of the first year I had four of these street houses. I had to put down a 25% deposit and pay capital and interest, so this left finances stretched. I looked at my 10- year plan and wondered how I would ever reach the 1 million pounds. I had now reached £80,000, I was proud of myself and just kept focused. However, I became a bit agitated, since when I did my sums again, I realised that to get to the 1 million using this method, I would have to buy 50 of these houses. The thought of 50 sets of tenants, with 50 kitchens and bathrooms to maintain, started to feel like a lot of hard work! I preferred quality to quantity but to buy a property more expensive would mean a bigger deposit and how could I raise this? I was going to have to think of something different. I was not sure HOW or WHY but all I knew was that I needed this million in property, and £20,000 street houses were not the way I wanted to go.

When on a buying trip for the boutique, to London, I heard of a girl who could not get her flat sold. She was pregnant and emigrating to the USA and needed to sell soon. This was all new to me; I didn't know anything about distressed sales. But I knew enough to work out that if she really wanted to sell and was sure of the sale, I could bargain with her. I asked if I could go and have a look at the flat.

When the appointment was secured, I called Ivan up and told him I'd has a hectic day buying stock for the shop and that I had missed my flight home but would catch one first thing in the morning.

That night I went to see her flat. It was a three-bedroom, spacious for London, in a decent area. I spoke with her and told her I had nothing to sell and had the money to buy it. Even thought I didn't have a loan offer, I knew I could get one. She was looking for £95,000 and I knew from speaking with the agent that I could get £300 per week in rent. I spent the night in the hotel working out figures. Using the same borrowing rates and deposit that I need for my previous properties I worked out that if I were able to get the house for £80,000 I could make the repayment, but it would be difficult and I would be under pressure to get together the 25% deposit. When I arrived home the next day after a couple of calls insuring I could get the loan money I put my offer in. By the end of that day she had accepted. I was now excited my plan was coming together, this was the type of thing I wanted to concentrate my energy on and one of these flats was equivalent to buying 4 street houses. Also there was a letting agency that would look after things for me.

Next, I really needed that 25% deposit which just seemed too much for me. I knew I was getting a bargain, and I was determined to get this flat. I remembered when Ivan and I had been in Spain for the weekend a few months prior that we had met a taxi driver and his wife and during dinner one night they told us that there friend was a mortgage broker. I looked for the driver's number and called him up, got his friend's number from him and made an appointment to go see him in London. It was a great day. The news was that I could now borrow 90%, so I only needed a 10% mortgage. My application was accepted and I was delighted. It was just up to me to get that £8,000 deposit. I managed to do so by cashing in an insurance policy I had taken out a couple of years prior. This came to £7,000- just one more thousand to get. I thought I might be able to take it out of cash flow from the shop, but that was a bit tight. I had a sleepless night or two, but when something is meant for you, everything always seems to fall in place. My mother arrived one evening to tell me that she was giving us all £1,000 out of my grandfather's estate. I was thrilled, to say the least. This solved a big problem for me; like everything in my life it always comes along when I need it most. Now I was able to move forward and get the flat.

Ivan and I flew to London the day after the sale of the flat closed. A couple of people were coming to view it. The second family that came said they were very interested in taking it, but asked if it would it be furnished. I asked if it needed to be, to which he replied, "Yes". This was 10am and our flight was leaving London Heathrow at 8pm. I called a taxi company and asked them to take us to some furniture shops close by. I went into the first shop and explained that I needed to furnish a house that very day and if I were to buy from them, could they deliver the furniture today?. When he replied yes, I immediately started to go around the shop picking out all the pieces I needed. Then I would ask him "What is the best price for this?" and I would get Ivan to write it down. I proceeded around the store in this manner until I had everything we needed. We left with the furniture all paid for, and the delivery was at 3pm. By 4.30pm the lease was signed and we were on our way to the airport.

Within a couple of months I was back in London doing the same thing again. This plan was working well. However, when I went to buy the third property, it was difficult. I was getting gazumped every time, and this was costing me money in solicitor's fees that I could not afford. The flats were going up by as much as £1000 per week. By end of 1999 my first flat was now worth £120,000. I was pleased but this was slowing me down.

Moving further still

For about a year I did not buy anything, as I could not afford to lose a bid. A friend of mine was buying in Dublin. I saw that this was not only a good market, but house values were growing and it was difficult to get the right house. It took me about six months to find something that I thought would work. This time I really pushed it, but I also realised that sometimes you have to take a risk, albeit calculated. I had watched my friend who was getting on well, and I knew that I could do it too.

This particular property was to cost me IR£340,000. The only problem was that it was not liveable, and it would cost another £100,000 to get it fixed up. I called up my bank and they put me in touch with their bank in Dublin, who said they would loan me the money, but I would have to come up with a deposit of £100,000. I decided I could do this by remortgaging my flats in London, which now had equity. I would also mortgage my shop and sell one of the houses in Portadown. I remember my accountant calling me in and asking me if I realised that if this did not work, I would be bankrupt. I replied that I was aware of the risk and I knew what I was doing, while fighting back tears of determination and anger at being challenged. I was buying this property, and I could see very clearly how I was doing it and how I would make it work. I was being very real and knew I would definitely have to keep focused to see this project through.

I managed to secure the property and get the deposit together. I remember the day I came out of the bank in Dublin onto the street. I was not sure if I was going to be sick or faint with fear. But deep down, I believed in myself and I recalled my grandmother's words: "Keep your chin up should your belly touch the ground." To be honest, it was feeling very close to the ground, and I knew the next few months were crucial!

I picked up the keys for the property on the 14th December 2000. The twins 12th Birthday and on the way home I stopped at the shop and bought a bottle of champagne. This was a huge achievement for me and I intended to celebrate it!

Now I had the keys in my hand the next challenge that was niggling in the back of my mind and gave me the sinking feeling was that I had not told Ivan the full extent of the work that needed to be done. Also, I had not let him view the property until I owned it. He had shown me over the years what to look for in a building, as he was an experienced builder. But as the property was old he would also be looking for problems that may never turn up, hence I felt the best thing for him to do was read the surveyors report. I felt the best way forward was to get the property bought, sort of like step one. Then, when we would have the keys in our hand and the property is legally ours, you have no choice but to get down to the work and get on with it (Step two). I think that in life it is about committing. When you are committed you just get on with it one step at a time.

On the Sunday we took our trip to Dublin, as we drove down the road towards the house, Ivan looked over at me and said, "Don't tell me it's one of these red-bricked Victorian houses," to which I made a slight nod and whispered a very quiet "Yes." He had known this prior but as it was not visual to him it had slipped his mind. Now the moment of truth was here and we were in front of it. However, when he had a look around he had to agree that structurally, it was sound; there would be a bit of work.

The next morning Ivan announced over breakfast that he didn't think that he could do the work in Dublin as he still worked in his fathers business and he would have no means to travel there. Prior to this Ivan would of worked within a 20 mile radius of our home, now this was almost 100miles away. I tried to clarify things, it seemed that the biggest issue was he had no van. When I got to the shop that morning I rushed upstairs, made a few calls, and popped out for a little while. When Ivan arrived home for dinner that night, I told him we had to hurry as we were going to the garage. I had got him a new van and all he had to do was pick which colour he liked best. I told him this would be his pay for the work he would do on the house.

Maintenance and Upkeep

Dublin at this time was two-and-a-half-hour drive from our house, and our refurbishing and maintenance went on for six months. Ivan would go to Dublin on a Monday, and stay until Wednesday, and then go back again on Thursday morning and stay until the weekend. It was a very busy time. I still had the shop and all the other properties and two children to juggle, but I knew it would not last forever and that we would get there. One day I was in a shop buying furniture for the house when the salesman said to me, "Let me write down this very important sentence of all two letter words" I gave him my cheque book and he wrote on the back of it "IF IT IS TO BE, IT IS UP TO ME." I loved it and have shared it with many over the years. When life feels tough, I just remind myself of this little sentence.

The house was divided into seven apartments. We started the refurbishment at the top of the house. As money was tight and I needed cash flow, as soon as a flat was ready, I would move Ivan into the one he was working on and rent the finished one. Slowly but surely, he made his way down the apartments until they were all complete. At the weekends I would go and paint in the apartments. Ivan's brothers were there, helping him too. As we neared the end of the project, we were all getting very tired, so to give us a goal, I booked a holiday for us on to the island of Madeira. It kept us alive knowing that soon we could crash out and relax. There were days that just seemed to run into each other and I was not sure what was going on. One thing was for sure: this project was a success, and by the time we had it completed, all the flats were rented.

By 2004 this house had doubled in price and I was amazed when I had to list my assets to find that at the age of 34 I had the one million pounds in property! It had been no easy road; it was about keeping focused and self-belief. There were times I wanted to lie down and cry with exhaustion or frustration, but you just have to pick yourself back up again. In comparison to everything else I had experienced these were all situations that you could just work through - with every now and then a temporary cash flow crisis.

I had promised myself that when I had the million pounds in property, I would buy myself a Mercedes car. I called at the garage one day to have a look at one, and then after the twins came home from school, I told them we were going on an adventure. I put them in the back of the new car and saw how they felt about it. I wanted to make sure they had enough legroom, they felt safe and if they liked the way it travelled on the road. They were excited and said it was really lovely. I was delighted it was a great success and after Ivan had a look at it, we agreed to buy this car. At the start I felt a bit guilty, but I loved my car. It was my little luxury, just for me and being automatic it took all the effort out of driving. After all it was me who was still driving 98 miles to Dublin and 98 miles home again every Tuesday night to sort out all the tenants at the house after working a full day at the shop.

Winds of Change are Coming

A couple of months after I closed the boutique, I bought a mobile home on the beach, just outside Cranfield on the Co. Down coast about 45 minutes drive from our house. It was a private site with about 500 mobile homes, a park and its own beach. Our mobile was located along the back wall with a view over the sea. It was idyllic. The twins and I lived there for all of July and August 2004. Ivan would come and stay at the weekends, and during the week I would just lounge around in the sun, relaxing on our patio and listening to the sounds of the seagulls and the twins playing with their new friends. At night I would leave my bedroom window open and drift off to sleep with the sound of the waves breaking on the beach. This calmed my soul and made me at peace with myself.

I really needed this time out to see where I was going. My Dad had just died in October 2003 and I had closed the shop in February 2004, "Lady R" had been my life, and in some ways my identity, but in this quiet relaxing space I was getting strong again.

When the twins went back to school in September 2004, I needed to do something more in property. After Ivan had returned from working at the house in Dublin he found it difficult to settle into his fathers building company again and wanted to do something himself. By June 2003 we had bought a one off building site and Ivan was in the process of constructing a new house to sell, as he had no wage coming in I decided I would go to the property auctions in London and see what was happening there. I had heard and looked in the auction guides and seen that you could buy commercial properties with a long lease, this would create an income for us. I visited first to get the feel of it and on returning the second time I was on a mission. I had earmarked a hotel to buy and had all my enquiries and the loan agreed.

The auction was in a very grand hotel in London. My tactic was to sit halfway up the room. It was a huge ballroom, with 500 or more people there. When the hotel that I was looking to buy came to the floor, I just watched at the early stages of the bidding, my heart started beating hard. Then when I started bidding, I think I stopped breathing. Finally the hammer went down and the auctioneer said, "Sold to the lady in the blue top." This was me! Within seconds there was a guy standing beside me with a piece of paper for me to sign plus he needed the deposit cheque. I felt myself shake slightly as I wrote out the deposit cheque. As I tore it out of my book, the Asian man sitting beside me leaned over and said, "You are a very clever lady." I looked at him and laughed with a reply "Come back and see me in five years and we will see" I got up and walked towards the back of the room and as I exited the room I realized that I was the only lady there. I went into the ladies' and called Ivan. When he picked up, I said, "Darling, we now own a hotel" he replied, "Roslyn, get off the phone - I am trying to dash a chimney." I was on my own, but this did not stop me celebrating my victory. I went into an Italian restaurant and ordered my favourite, spaghetti bolognaise, and a big glass of red wine to celebrate. Within four weeks the property was mine and on closing day as the lease was already in place, I received my first rent. This was simple I thought.

Two months later I was back again at the auction, and this time I bought a pub by the same means. It was again rented out, and when the sale closed in four weeks I got the first rent cheque.

Although I was far beyond my dream, I was slightly unsettled and still looking for something. Although this way brought me more income, it did not appear to satisfy my soul. I needed something that I could be creative with, to give me a purpose again.

KNOWING WHEN ENOUGH IS ENOUGH

Shortly after this, I was asked to look at a property in Chester. When I arrived in this city, I had no idea what it was like. I went in search of the property, and when I stepped into this street in the heart of the old city, I fell in love with it. I had never seen anything like it. The buildings were black and white Tudor style. On each side of the street there was an upper balcony, one shop on top of the other, which you can walk, within the walls of this Roman city. These double rows of shops are called "The Rows." I thought it was magical, and I really wanted to buy something here. I was not sure why, but there was an air of culture and class and it felt good for me. On investigating, I realised that this was a small city with great opportunities.

The first property I looked at, I was outbid on. Within a couple of weeks the agent came back to me and said that someone had approached him to see if he knew the under bidder and if they would be interested in looking at his property. I flew over to Chester and had a look at it. WOW! The two shops were rented out on long lease to the hairdresser Toni & Guy but it was the upper floors that intrigued me. They had not been lived in for over 100 years. I was excited because I saw what I could do with this. I would make living accommodation in the upstairs. Also at the back there was a tiny building divided over three floors that I could restore and make into a cottage.

Eventually we agreed on a price, and the building was mine. This I knew would be my last project. I had gone beyond my wildest dreams and I knew that when I completed this, I was fulfilled. It took two years to get the planning approval as the property was listed inside and out. Then it took 15 months to get the work complete. I hired a project management team for this because of the logistics and the size of the job. During the first part of the project, I would fly over every month and liase with the team. When the work finally began, Ivan and I would both fly over every month until the work was complete.

As this project was coming to an end, in Summer 2007, the property market was going crazy. It had gone from not enough supply to over-saturation. When the apartments were finally completed, in July 2007 I managed to get the first two rented, and then after a few months the third, by Christmas 2007 I still had not got the last apartment rented. I just could not understand why. Unlike the new apartments, these were beautiful, full of character and charm, and the views from the lounge area were unique, down over this old street and "The Rows."

Intuition and devine guidance

One day when Ivan and I were staying at the apartment, we were chatting and he said, "I think you have pushed it all a bit too far." He then got up and went outside to empty the bin. I stood up and looked out the window, feeling very low and thinking maybe he was right. I said out loud "God if I ever need you, I need you right now, show me what to do with this property" I always feel that I am divinely guided. When I looked down I saw all these people standing just outside my shops. Just then I realised they were tourists, and then I remembered that my shops used to be "Barlow's," the oldest pub in Chester and these were tourists on a walking tour. By the time Ivan returned I was all excited again and could hardly get the words out. I said to him that I was going to make the apartments into holiday lets. On the way home that day I could not stop talking about it. I was so excited - I just knew it would work.

The next day I called the Chester tourist board and in my ignorance I asked if there was such a thing as a self-catering department. I was quickly put through to a man who told me all about setting up the business. He also gave me the names of a couple of people already doing this. He mentioned that there would be a meeting the following week showing you how to make your place acceptable to the criteria. I asked him if there were any places left.

The following week we were back in Chester to see how to get an accreditation for our property. I had not a clue how to do this or how I was going to get bookings. All I knew was that it felt right I would just have to make the commitment, and all the other things would fall into place.

Within a month I had a web site, credit card terminal in my office to accept payments, and an appointment for the accreditation. It was not long until the bookings started to arrive. I put in safes so people with the aid of the code could retrieve their key on arrival.

I found a professional cleaning company. Finally we got the tourist board rating of four stars. I was thrilled! This was a business I could run very easily, and over the next couple of years, as the long-term tenants left I converted each apartment into holiday/business lets. I named the place Commonhall Apartments. It was a great labour of love restoring this old building, and I feel it was a great honour to be able to buy the building and restore it. Most of all, it gives me great pleasure to share it with people from all over the world. I love to visit and see their comments in the visitors' books. When I call to see whether they have arrived and they are excited and say things such as, "The place is just wonderful and a real home away from home, with a fabulous location" it gives me great pleasure to feel like I am doing something worthwhile.

When I first set up the holiday business, Ivan asked me what we were going to do if something went wrong and we were back home in Ireland. To which I replied it would all be Ok. Things will be fine. You see, to me my life has been like driving on a foggy road - only seeing the first 100 yards, but knowing when I would get past that 100 yards I would be able to see the next 100 yards. You don't need to know everything. You just need to know enough to get you to the next 100 yards. Anyhow, no sooner had I started thinking about how would I overcome a logistic obstacle, when an invitation arrived, to an "Open Evening" with the Chester tourist board. It was during this meeting that we met Roger and Jill Maher. They own "The Courtyard" in Helsby, a few miles outside of Chester. We had a lot in common, as they too have beautiful holiday-let cottages that they also had resorted in the courtyard where they lived. They were local and had very good contacts for all the small things that can become a problem, and they even offered to hold a key to our property.

Roger and Jill invited us to come and view their place. The first time we visited them, we felt as if we had known them all our lives. They are now our very dear friends, and of course when we are full we recommend them to guests and they do likewise.

Chester is full of little alleys and hidden places and soon another lady decided to open her cottage that she had just converted to holiday lets. As Roger and Jill had helped me, it gave me great pleasure to help Sandra with her beautiful cottage, "Watergatenook".

We are all like a little family, and although we live in Ireland, and fly over and visit our property once per month. I have connected with these wonderful people in this magical City.

Entering a New Stage

I dearly love going to Chester and seeing all the new friends I have made there. When I bought this property, I knew in my heart that this would be my last one, because I had reached my wildest dreams and beyond. I had a sense of satisfaction with my properties and take my responsibilities to my tenants very serious. I know each one by name and they have my contact number. The families that live and run the hotel and the pub know me also and I work along with them, helping them with my experience and business acumen any way I can, however for me personally, I had pushed myself outside my comfort zone and felt I had gotten to the top of Everest to discover there was really only snow. Again, I was restless and not really sure what it was that would make me feel whole. There was one thing I was sure of, that this: more, better, best, more, better, best, was not what I was looking for. I had reached all my goals and more, but still felt empty inside, so the question was "now what?"

CHAPTER 10

Reflections on my Journey

Reaching the Peak

I was now age 41. I realised that I had no plan for the rest of my life. I had always said I would be grateful to live to 40, and now it had come and gone. I had achieved everything on the outside, but inside I felt empty. I had reached all the goals I had given myself, beyond my biggest dreams, and for the second time in my life I realized that I did not know who I was. This time it had nothing to do with physically or emotional trauma. This time, I had been working so hard I lost myself. I was busy caring for the children, my husband, keeping house and enjoying business success. But was this really success, this empty trail of never ending work?

Then I read that success means successful living. When you are peaceful, happy and doing what you love to do, and then you are successful. That sounded a bit more like it. I didn't think that my achievements made me any better than anyone else, I never judge anyone and would help anyone in anyway I can. Hadn't society told me when I became a successful businessperson with the supportive husband, kids, lovely home, and car that I would feel great, but there was something still missing I still wasn't complete. I was looking for inner peace and something to make me feel alive again, the twins were now 19 years old, I was starting to feel redundant as a mother, had a little bit more time to myself to think and wondering what all my life had been about. Once again, another challenge was put before me and, as in the past I rose to the occasion.

Ivan and I were invited to go on a two-day Seminar, delivered by Tom McNally, from Derrynoose, Co. Armagh. This course I thought initially was a personal development course, but it transpired to be a deeply moving and spiritually enlightening experience.

I thought it would be a good idea for us both to attend as I felt Ivan needed more confidence to move forward. I was sure that I didn't really need to go but I would to keep him company and pick up some nugget of information. This was to be a self-revelation to me, because when we got there, I learned that your thoughts control your life. Looking back at how I dealt with the trauma of the accident I could certainly agree. I could also agree on the business side: oh yes, anything I wanted to do in business, I just did. But there was something more; an inner box that had been opened that could not be closed. I had this yearning for inner peace.

What Coaching Taught Me

I immersed myself in audios and books on motivation, inspiration and self-help. Then I went to see Jack Canfield Co- Author of Chicken Soup for the Soul books, at a conference he was holding in Dublin. I spoke to him before the seminar began and asked him for his autograph for a friend who really admired him. He asked me about myself, and when he went onstage he told of meeting a lady earlier who had been in a serious car accident and had got her life back together and became successful. I could feel myself sinking into the seat, as I knew it was me he was talking about. My friend who was with me told me to give myself credit for my achievements as they had obviously made an impression on Jack for him to talk about me on stage. During the day he made us set our goals, and everyone around me was looking for money. I thought this was really sad and wanted to say, No, it is not what you are looking for, what you really want is inner contentment and happiness to Love and be loved.

On the way out of the seminar my friend introduced me to a girl who was a life coach. She said that she would meet me for a one-to-one coaching day. I took her card and called her up in the next couple of days and made an appointment.

I arrived at her apartment and she told me this was my special day, just for me, and to turn my phone off. I almost collapsed, and said, "What, turn my phone off? You must be joking because everybody will be looking for me! She said that was my problem. I had spoiled everyone or let them be dependent on me. She said, "What can happen in a few hours that cannot be sorted out? Give yourself time out." As I never give myself time out, I agreed reluctantly, but instead I put my phone on silent, so I could see if anyone was looking for me. We went through all the painful parts of my life. I had one of those crying uncontrollably afternoons with her telling me I was allowing everyone else to take over my life and jumping to their attention. Inside, I firmly disagreed. After all I thought this girl was 40 – a couple of years younger than me – and had no children or husband. What did she know about having a hectic life? I thanked her and hugged her as I was leaving.

When I got to my car I saw there were 48 missed calls. I was almost sick. Maybe this girl was right; everyone truly did depend on me. Or had I allowed everyone to depend on me? That day made me realize that I loved everyone and gave so much, but I had forgotten about myself. I had forgotten to love myself. I felt guilty for taking time out for me, and then I realised if you don't love yourself, you start to feel empty because you are always giving. When you feel empty it builds up frustration and a feeling of worthlessness, which results in anger and resentment. I understood that it is not selfish to love yourself because if you give away all your love, there is nothing left for yourself. The realisation hit me like a bolt of lightening. I had given all of myself to my business, my children and my husband. I realised that I am worthy of being loved and that I will never feel a true sense of self-worth until I love myself.

I discovered during this time that we are like computers. Our subconscious mind is like the hard drive of a computer, storing information, and our conscious mind is like the keyboard, always punching in everything we see and what is being said around us and to us. Every now and then we need to look at the information we have been given and update ourselves by removing the old programming or conditioning. In Ireland girls are brought up to be giving, we watch our mothers and grandmothers who were told to give men preference, feed and look after everyone and then yourself. Unfortunately, this is not the correct method, it is a conditioning handed down generation after generation, slightly diluted each time, but still the same message. As a car cannot run on empty, a woman cannot feel fulfilled without self-love. It was time to update my computer.

Meditation and Relaxation

During this time of self-discovery, I took a class in relaxation and meditation. At the start it was very difficult for me to switch my brain off. Each week I would go into the class determined but the more I tried the more active my mind seemed to become – it was frustrating. I had wanted so badly to have this time to switch off. After a few weeks I was managing to get about 5 minutes before the class was about to end, but then gradually week after week it started to build to 10 minutes and soon I could still the full hour. It is like everything in life it takes practice and you have to learn.

My cousin then called me up and asked me if I would go to a Reiki class with her. At this class the healing started, I could switch off and reunite my mind and my body. It was a fabulous feeling and made me feel whole. The teacher taught us about energy and how we could heal ourselves and establish a link with our spirit guides and creator. It was great and my energy now seemed to flow. I completed the first two levels of Reiki healing and then I was introduced to Integrated Energy Therapy to which I completed levels one, two and three. This took me to a higher level, a level that opened up my sixth sense. I recognised that I had been using this in my business world and knew instinctively if I could trust someone or would want to do business with them. Now I was learning to use it in my everyday life. To turn off the emotions that drag you down and put your energy on the emotions that lift you up.

When you activate your sixth sense, it is like opening up your life energy, giving you a sense of freedom and power from within. You start observing subtle energy, how people around you make you feel, what gives you harmony in your life and you join in the synchronistic flow of life. It will not give you all the answers in advance but you know that no matter what situation arrives in your life you will have the tools to deal with it. When you meet people they start to notice you, as your light shining out from within gives you a charisma that attracts people to you and as they chat with you they cannot help but walk away feeling good. They have unknowingly tapped into your vibration. It is like you are passing love around to peoples subconscious and I think if everyone in the world was like this wouldn't it be a great place.

In the past two years in my quest, I have come to realize that I was not a victim of anything that happened to me. Instead these challenges have become my gifts, as I can now go forward to inspire, uplift and show others by my example. Your darkest days can be your greatest gifts and your sources of great learning. You are not alone; the sun is always shining on you. It is just that no one ever told you that you had your back turned.

I was truly amazed that people felt my life to this point had been extraordinary; it was a big revelation to me and extremely humbling. I really felt sure that my life was no different than anyone else's. However, I now realise it is not what happens to you that matters, but how you react to it. My journey now is to help others rise and get through their challenges by using my own life as example.

Through writing about my own life, I have come to realise that life is a journey, one made up of small trips. An ultimate goal of material, financial or external success is not really what your life is about. Your life is really a succession of little victories, and it is in these little victories that you make your success. It is not about the big catch "at the end." If you get to what you thought "the end" was, you just keep moving the goalposts and again think when I get –when I get- When I get. You will never achieve satisfaction. So you have to start learning to celebrate your little victories on your journey of life and love yourself for the here and now, to be grateful and thankful for everything that comes your way. Then you will become at one with yourself and feel whole.

I am grateful and thankful for every experience my life has given me so far. I live in the state of gratitude and helping others as much as I can. I realise that there are people you are supposed to meet, people who will come into your life for a reason. Sometimes they will stay a little while, and sometimes they will stay a lifetime. You have to be grateful and thankful for the time that you have with them and for the lessons they teach you, as well as for what you share, and give to each other in order to grow.

Life is all about choices. Sometimes they are painful, but you have to make them because that is part of your process or enlightenment. It is part of what shapes, moulds and makes you. They are your lessons on life and you are here to learn them. When you make a decision that is right for you, in your stomach will get that gut feeling, that knowing feeling. When you listen to yourself, you are taking responsibility for yourself and your power. No one owes you anything in this life but you. Make your own choices! These are your gifts to yourself. Sometimes they are painful, and we often have to let go of something smaller to make a void for something greater to arrive. Deep down inside, we all have our answers to all the things that have and will happen to us in this life, as we have already agreed to undertake the journey before we even got here. If you feel scared and don't know what to do just give yourself a little time out to sit quietly and meditate, listen to your heart. The word "ear" is in heart, so listen, to your heart, as deep inside you will have the answers you will know if you are doing something right or wrong for you. You owe it to yourself to listen for the answers that will ease your journey on this path, look for that life you were destined to live with all your unique talents that you were given and because of conditioning you have buried deep inside. We are all born unique beautiful beings, with great talents and have our own unique contributions that we need to give while we are here and fulfil our role of significance.

It takes a lot of courage to reach out and take your responsibility and whenever you do there will be times when fear tries to over come you but at this time you need to give yourself a little self praise by reflecting on how far you have come and knowing you are always safe and protected. Soon by connecting to your inner self you will start to glow from the inside out as you are on your path and the knowing feeling arrives within. You will let go of the fear and you start to relax, as all seems to fit perfectly into place.

As I wrote this book and looking back over my life, I realised that when I got married I thought that Ivan was my prince and he would rescue me from all the traumas of life. But what truly made me strong was not that the prince rescued me. But my faith, courage, and determination to pick myself up and become grateful for the wonderful life I had been given. In other words I was the administrator of my own rescue as no one can save us but ourselves.

Most of all this journey of life is about LOVE. We all need to be loved to the centre of our being so we can shine our light upon the world. But no matter how much love is poured upon you by someone else until you love yourself, you will not be able to feel it. You must give yourself time to connect with and love yourself.

I am giving you the gift of my story. By opening my heart and pouring out my journey, I hope that I am inspiring you to live your life to your potential. You deserve to love and appreciate yourself and create your dream.

This will be your greatest achievement as it was mine. I have come to realise that all the worldly riches of money and possessions cannot bring you close to anything like the inner peace and joy you can have if you just take that time to find out who you are and love yourself. We are all incapable of being loved if we do not love ourselves.

We are like mirrors always reflecting back what we are giving out. It is a must to love ourselves first, so when our body overflows with love and we naturally exude love from a deeper level. It is easy to give when you have abundance.

This is the true gift of love.

This is true success and this is real life!

Roslyn x